With every good wish for Christmas and for the
New Year.

The Colcocks

Florence, Alabama
December 1970

*"The lines are fallen unto me in pleasant places,
yea, I have a goodly heritage."*

Psalms XV, 4

ALABAMA

ART CONSULTANT
Max Heldman
PRODUCTION ART
Karl Scott

EDITORIAL ASSISTANTS
Annie Bestor Mitchell
Mabel G. Rowley
Azilee M. Weathers

HERITAGE

by Virginia Pounds Brown and Helen Morgan Akens

The Strode Publishers
Huntsville, Alabama

Preface

This book is an attempt in words and pictures to take a longer and wider view of Alabama history. Frequently we have been too concerned with our social and political activities for the past one hundred years, and too little aware that Alabama has cradled civilizations from the Ice Age to the Space Age.

The habits, peculiarities, regional trends, similarities, and common heritage are woven into this Alabama story. Recent developments in archaeological methods reveal that the great caves of Alabama sheltered prehistoric people, and that the largest population of Indians in the Southeast in the sixteenth, seventeenth, and eighteenth centuries lived on Alabama's rivers. Only recently have our scholars properly examined the archives of Europe where our colonial heritage is best recorded. Their findings reveal the important role that Alabama played in shaping our country's destiny when European powers fought for possession of the Southeast.

As new information has become evident, the importance of the rivers of Alabama and the rich bottom lands that the rivers made has become increasingly evident. The drama of Alabama history has been played in this river system.

We have chosen to conclude this book with the Civil War, turning point in Alabama history as in so much of the nation. Perhaps the best evidence still extant of the old South is the antebellum homes. We have tried to select houses of many different architectural types and from throughout Alabama. We realize that we have given no more than a passing salute to the many fine homes still standing but trust that we have chosen those representative of the state.

It is particularly difficult in a book of this type to properly acknowledge all the assistance which we have received from so many sources. We have worked in many libraries, but we are particularly indebted to the Southern Collection of the Birmingham Public Library, the Huntsville Public Library, and the Alabama Department of Archives and History. This book would not have been possible without the cooperation of historical societies, chambers of commerce, newspapers, and numerous individuals.

The source of each picture used in this book has been acknowledged with the picture. We have done this not only to recognize the source but to locate important pictorial material of Alabama history. We have used "courtesy of" when the picture has been loaned or given to us. Numerous photographers, both professional and amateur, have contributed to the compiling of material. The five hundred pictures included have been selected from many more hundreds examined during the four years in which this book has been compiled. The final selection of the pictures to be used has depended in some cases upon their historical rather than their pictorial quality.

If, as is said, man studies the past in order to know the present and the future, the understanding of Alabama's rich heritage will help us better understand the Alabamians of today and tomorrow.

Virginia Pounds Brown
Helen Morgan Akens

Table of Contents

Introduction

Extensive pictorial histories have been published, at least as early as the time of William Cullen Bryant and Justin Winsor, and individual titles have often contained distinguished illustrative matter, sometimes even in color, such as the material of Thomas L. McKenney and James Hall. While Alabama has not been as fortunate in pictorial publications as some other states, nevertheless numerous histories of Alabama have been illustrated, and sometimes with striking pictures. Yet when all examples are cited, it is still true that *Alabama Heritage* is the first full-length history of Alabama which is profusely illustrated. In seeking out, collecting, identifying, arranging systematically and publishing this pictorial story of Alabama, Helen Morgan Akens and Virginia Pounds Brown have performed proudly. Just thumb through this fascinating pictorial history of Alabama and each of us will get a different but a very good introduction to the arresting pictures and trenchant sentences which illuminate its pages. These authors make an articulate team.

The story of *Alabama Heritage* runs from rock hounds in Scottsboro and Decatur to the sack of Selma and the Surrender; it moves from Eufaula to Tuscaloosa and from Mobile southward to Bellingrath Gardens, northward to Mooresville and eastward to the Big Spring. Selections, in other words, are representative of Alabama history in both time and space. Archaeologists are shown using the radioactive carbon-14 method at Russell Cave and the Quad site near Decatur. Indian progress is covered from the Paleo to the Mound Builders. Notable is the picture of the "rattle snake" disc, bought from a plow-hand by Dr. Eugene Allen Smith, and also the famous Crested Duck Bowl, discovered by Dr. Clarence A. Moore. The dramatic paintings by Jacques Le Moyne, often called the earliest pictures of America, now unhappily vanished save for one single item, nevertheless survive in the engravings of Theodore de Bry and furnish several pictures for *Alabama Heritage*. More generous are samplings of Alabama Indians as portrayed by the redoubtable Thomas L. McKenney, James Hall and Charles Byrd King. Examples are famous portraits of Sequoya, Paddy Carr, Jim Boy, Yoholomicco and many other Alabama-connected Indian portraits, which once hung in the Smithsonian Institution.

I like the pictures and prose concerning Spaniards and Frenchmen in colonial Alabama: the story of the Le Moyne brothers carving out a gallic empire in the Alabama wilderness and the stories of those who were pathetically loyal to the improbable George III amidst the failure of the first British Empire, under the not-too-severe blows of resurgent Spain, Charles III, and Bernardo Gálvez.

In picture and prose much of Alabama history passes in review, glamorous, dangerous, beautiful, prosperous and tragic, but with few examples of everyday drabness. Here we see pioneer life, cotton, slaves, stagecoaches (like the one drawn by Captain Basil Hall), steamboats, railroads, industries, plantations, churches, schools, abstract ideas, arts, and, too, even then there was politics. (I like especially pictures from *Remember Mobile* written by Caldwell Delaney.)

Also there is the story of Yancey and Secession, of Union invasion of the Tennessee Valley, the Battle of Mobile Bay (it is too bad the Smithsonian did not get *Tecumseh* out of the water in time to add to the coverage of the Battle of Mobile Bay in *Alabama Heritage*), and the elaborate and prolonged land campaign of Mobile of which Wilson's famous raid was a dramatic part. So here is *Alabama Heritage*.

Acknowledgements on the art work comprise in themselves interesting insights into rich resources of Alabama history.

Charles Grayson Summersell
History Department Chairman
University of Alabama

University, Alabama
September 15, 1967

FIRST
ALABAMIANS

United States Department of Interior, National Park Service

*Entrance to Russell Cave, prehistoric man's
oldest known home in the Southeast.*

THEY DISCOVERED ALABAMA

Indian artifacts are scattered across Alabama in numbers too great to count. "The tribes that slumber" have left their mark from cave shelters on river bluffs to the great earthen pyramids of Moundville. Throughout the state pottery fragments, projectiles and shell ornaments point to ancient villages, campsites, and hunting and burial grounds.

Archeologists try to separate these prehistoric people by their types of culture. The things they made determined to a great extent the way they lived. Four successive occupations by different prehistoric Indian groups in Alabama extended roughly from about 10,000 B.C. to 1500 A.D. These periods are known as Paleo-Indian, Archaic, Woodland, and Mound Builder.

The first inhabitants of Alabama were hunters of the Paleo-Indian period. Archeologists believe that they came into Alabama during the last Ice Age. Traveling in small bands, these hunters pursued herds of prehistoric animals such as the now extinct mammoths, mastodons, and hairy elephants. In this last Ice Age period much of North America was still covered by a great ice mass, but in Alabama, as in the rest of the South, the ice had melted and grassy plains had begun to appear. As these herds of animals moved southward, they drifted into the Tennessee river valley to graze. Close behind them came the nomadic hunters who camped where the big game was plentiful, moving on when the animals migrated or became extinct.

Until recently archeologists could only estimate how long ago these Ice Age hunters roamed Alabama. With the atomic age, however, came the knowledge that all living organisms contain a radioactive carbon. This radioactivity begins to decay when the plant or animal dies. With the use of a Geiger counter to determine the amount of radioactivity, charcoal from ancient campfires as well as other organic material can be dated. Archeologists have used this method, known as carbon-14 dating, at Alabama's two most important prehistoric

archeological sites, Russell Cave and the Quad site near Decatur. At the Quad site excavators have unearthed one of the earliest types of fluted spear point, the Clovis Point, named for a place in Arizona where the first one was found. Ice Age hunters used such points to kill big game. Archeologists have established by carbon-14 dating and types of spear points that the earliest people to inhabit the New World came into the Southern regions of North America, and that the Tennessee valley of Alabama sheltered many of these first people.

As large game became scarce, the nomadic hunters disappeared, and a more settled people who lived on small game, nuts, and fruits migrated into this region. These Indians, known as Archaic, were attracted to the many streams of Alabama, where they found abundant supplies of mussels and fish. They built their campsites beside these streams. Mounds of discarded oyster and clam shells mark the site of Archaic Indians in Alabama.

About 8000 B.C. Archaic man faded from Alabama's past, and a third group, the Woodland Indians, appeared. Gradually important changes took place in the Woodland Indians' way of living. No longer were they dependent upon animals for food; by this time they had established a well-defined agricultural life. Villages became larger and more permanent. Time and energy could be spent on the arts because there was now an assured food supply. These Indians developed weaving and made pottery for cooking and other purposes. Such pottery fragments, called potsherd, found throughout Alabama, are one of the archeologists' most helpful research tools for recreating the life of these Indians.

The last of the prehistoric Indian groups in Alabama were the Mound Builders. Apparently as the Woodland culture developed throughout the Southeast, there emerged from it the highly civilized Mound Builders, who left Alabama its first permanent monuments—the earthen pyramids.

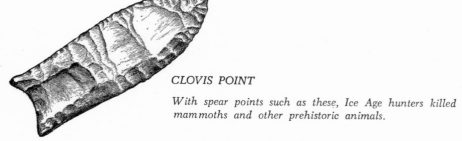

CLOVIS POINT

With spear points such as these, Ice Age hunters killed mammoths and other prehistoric animals.

This cave scene depicts family life as it was among the prehistoric Indians in Alabama thousands of years ago. The man is making a dart-throwing stick, called an "atlatl," his most important weapon. A Stone Age axe and a knife lie within easy reach. A fish is cooking over the fire in the rear of the cave while the boy appears to be fashioning tools from bones. The woman sews on a leather garment; an awl made from bone rests on her knee. A baby sleeps strapped to a cradleboard.

Archaic man's
WEAPONS and TOOLS

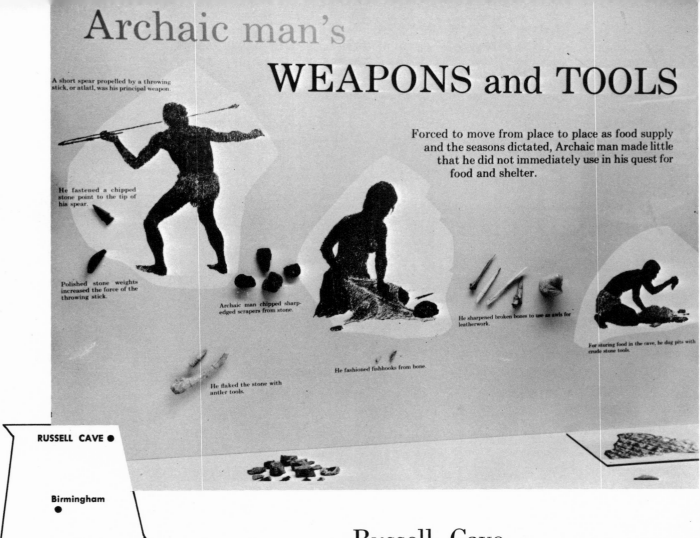

A short spear propelled by a throwing stick, or atlatl, was his principal weapon.

He fastened a chipped stone point to the tip of his spear.

Polished stone weights increased the force of the throwing stick.

Archaic man chipped sharp-edged scrapers from stone.

He flaked the stone with antler tools.

He fashioned fishhooks from bone.

He sharpened broken bones to use as awls for leatherwork.

For storing food in the cave, he dug pits with crude stone tools.

Forced to move from place to place as food supply and the seasons dictated, Archaic man made little that he did not immediately use in his quest for food and shelter.

RUSSELL CAVE ●

Birmingham ●

Montgomery ●

Mobile ●

Russell Cave

When a powerline employee picked up several points near Bridgeport, in northeast Alabama, he began a chain of events which led to the discovery of Russell Cave, one of the most important archeological discoveries in North America. Russell Cave is primitive man's oldest known home in the Southeast. As archeologists sifted and analyzed handful after handful of dirt, Russell Cave told its remarkable story of continuous use from about 10,000 B.C. to the colonial period of American history.

The large caves with overhanging rocks typical of the Tennessee valley area attracted prehistoric men. Russell Cave was an ideal place in which to live. It was 107 feet wide and 27 feet high, and was also dry, with fresh water outside at the foot of the hillside and game abounding nearby. These were all assets to primitive man who needed sim-

ple shelter, protection from his enemies, and food to hunt.

It is to the women, however, that we are indebted for the treasures of Russell Cave. These housekeepers of long ago were unbelievably messy. Instead of ridding the cave of rubbish they simply covered it with dirt. Protected from rain, erosion, silt, and flood these layers of rubbish grew intensely higher.

Not until 1953 was this remarkable timetable of human existence explored and made known to the world. Then the National Geographic Society purchased the 262-acre farm on which Russell Cave is located. The society sent a professional archeologist, Carl Miller, to explore the cave. In 1961 the National Geographic Society presented the deed of the site to the Interior Department for the establishment of the Russell Cave National Monument.

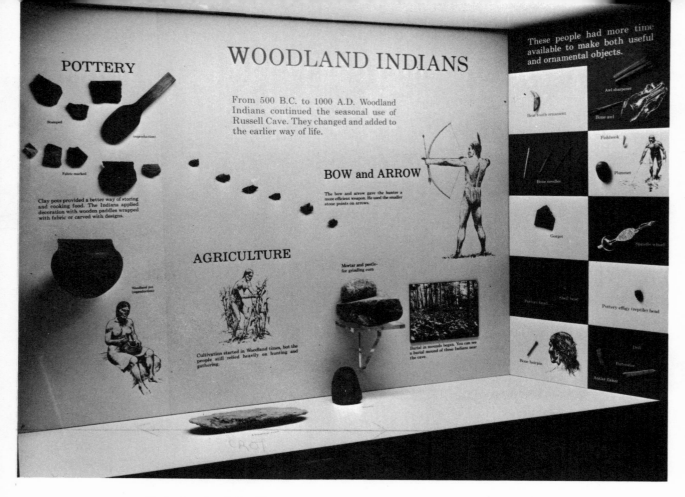

POTTERY

Stamped

(reproductions)

Fabric-marked

Clay pots provided a better way of storing and cooking food. The Indians applied decoration with wooden paddles wrapped with fabric or carved with designs.

Woodland pot (reproduction)

WOODLAND INDIANS

From 500 B.C. to 1000 A.D. Woodland Indians continued the seasonal use of Russell Cave. They changed and added to the earlier way of life.

BOW and ARROW

The bow and arrow gave the hunter a more efficient weapon. He used the smaller stone points on arrows.

AGRICULTURE

Cultivation started in Woodland times, but the people still relied heavily on hunting and gathering.

Mortar and pestle for grinding corn

Burial in mounds began. You can see a burial mound of these Indians near the cave.

These people had more time available to make both useful and ornamental objects.

Bear tooth ornament — *Awl sharpener* — *Bone awl* — *Fishhook* — *Plummet* — *Bone needles* — *Gorget* — *Spindle wheel* — *Pottery bead* — *Shell bead* — *Pottery effigy (reptile) head* — *Bone hairpin* — *Drill* — *Perforator* — *Antler flaker*

Displays from Russell Cave Museum, United States Department of Interior, National Park Service

ADVANCED FARMERS

After 1000 A.D., the Indians built large permanent villages in the rich bottomlands. Intensive agriculture supported a larger and more stable population.

The Indians made pottery in a variety of sizes and shapes.

They wore copper-covered wooden earspools in pierced ears.

Shell ornaments bore elaborate religious symbols.

One such village stood on the banks of the Tennessee River, 10 miles south of Russell Cave. These objects were excavated there by the University of Alabama.

Flint blade

They made and decorated pipes for the ceremonial smoking of tobacco.

while at Russell Cave

These arrowheads and pottery fragments reflect the occasional use of Russell Cave by the Advanced Farmers.

Until 1839 this was Cherokee territory. This handmade iron fishhook may have been dropped in the cave by a Cherokee or an early settler.

In the early morning hours the group loads for the dig.

This photograph taken in 1911 shows a group of Alabamians posing in front of an Indian mound which they have been excavating. Seated in the center is Dr. Thomas McAdory Owen, head of the Alabama Department of Archives and History. Under his leadership the department, first of its kind in the United States, assembled an outstanding collection of Alabama Indian artifacts.

Digging Up Alabama's Past

"Anybody can dig up things; but it is only by observation and interpretation that we can dig up the past." Sir Leonard Woolley.

Underway here is an "amateur dig" supervised by the Alabama Archeological Society. The site has been laid off in five-foot squares and each bit of dirt is being examined, sifted, and marked with the number of the square from which it was removed. In the right foreground is a typical prehistoric burial. The arms and legs of the corpse have been folded and bound to the body. Personal possessions such as shell ornaments are found in many of these graves.

6

Inside Cathedral Caverns at Grant archeologists are excavating the cave. The entrance is 128 feet long and 60 feet high. Many Indian artifacts have been found here.

MYSTERY OF THE MOUNDS

The forty great earthen pyramids of Moundville rise impressively from 315 acres of flatland. To view these pyramids is to look back into prehistoric times when an advanced Indian culture flourished on this spot between 1200 A.D. and 1600 A.D. Here is Alabama's most visible link with her prehistoric Indians. Working in this rich, black soil, archeologists have unearthed at Moundville the largest religious center of the Mound Builder people in the eastern Mississippi valley. Moundville served as a religious mecca for a group of small villages scattered over a wide area in a loose confederation typical of the Mound Builder culture.

Before the Civil War this land was part of the cotton plantation of the Prince family, who had a fine collection of Indian pipes plowed up in the fields. Not until 1905, however, when the Philadelphia Academy of Natural Science sent Dr. Clarence A. Moore to work the site, did a systematic excavation of Moundville begin. Dr. Moore with his team of archeologists operated from a barge on the Warrior river. Each morning they climbed the steep bluff for the day's dig, and each night on the barge the lamps burned late as Dr. Moore recorded and analyzed the day's findings. Dr. Moore's most exciting discovery was the crested duck bowl, considered one of the finest prehistoric Indian artifacts in America. He was digging in a burial pit at Moundville about sixteen inches from the surface and had just unearthed a skeleton and an effigy pipe shaped like a dog when he made his remarkable find. Concerning this, Dr. Moore wrote to his colleagues in Philadelphia:

> "Alongside this pipe and projecting beyond it, was what seemed to be a sharp fragment of stone. This fragment proved to be part of the rim of a large bowl from which projected upward a beautifully carved arching neck and head of a crested duck, evidently the drake of the wood duck. Part of the crest is missing. Some distance away in the same pit lying on its side just below the surface of the ground was the rest of the bowl to which the duck head belonged. On the head and neck of the duck, on the conventional tail and body of the vessel, is incized decoration executed with wonderful accuracy . . . The missing part of the crest of the duck was vainly sought by five men who for several hours passed between their fingers all material that had been thrown from the excavation."

Just who these Moundville Indians were and from whence they came is shrouded in mystery. They lived in houses made from logs and poles, weatherproofed with reeds, and plastered with sand and clay. Swamp grass waterproofed the roof, and a hole in the center served as a chimney. The Mound Builders were farmers, raising corn, beans, pumpkins, and tobacco. Most of their food was cultivated, but they did some hunting and fishing.

The Mound Builders developed the art of molding and carving to a greater degree than any other North American Indian. Moundville is particularly famous for the excellent quality of its ceremonial pottery, used in the religious and burial customs of the sun-worshiping Indians. Ceremonial disks or gorgets have been found at Moundville in greater numbers, in larger sizes, and with more elaborate engravings than any others so far uncovered. These disks, part of the burial ritual, may have been placed around the neck of the dead to ward off evil spirits. The rattlesnake disk is a famous example of the typical symbols used by the Moundville Indians. Such symbols included the sun circle, the human hand and eye, and entwined serpents—favorite symbols also of the Mexican Indians. Drinking vessels and pipes made in the likeness of a human figure were frequently buried with the dead.

The Moundville Indians appeared and disappeared as mysteriously as the earlier Indians of the Paleo, Archaic, and Woodland era. Some archeologists think that the Mound Builders represent the outer fringes of a civilization in which the more sophisticated Mayas, Toltecs, and Aztecs flourished. Like these more advanced people, the Moundville Indians were a sun-worshiping cult. All of them practiced many of the same religious rituals. Strikingly similar to the stone and cement temples in Mexico are the Moundville earthen pyramids and their wood and thatch superstructures. Because the Indians of the Southwest show an altogether different and less advanced culture than the Mound Builders, archeologists believe that Mexican influence may have spread across the Gulf of Mexico from Yucatan rather than overland.

Whatever the origin of the Mound Builders, the fact remains that these people spread their culture from the Gulf coast up the Mississippi valley almost to the Great Lakes. Moundville, on the Warrior river, was the center of the branch which spread eastward from the Mississippi river. Today thousands of visitors come annually to visit Moundville and its prehistoric area, preserved much as it was hundreds of years ago.

Mound State Monument

The mounds and the story of the people who built them are preserved today at Mound State Monument.

Museum of the American Indian, Heye Foundation

Crested Duck Bowl

This bowl, a stylized likeness of a crested wood duck, is one of the most prized Indian artifacts in this country; it has been called the "Portland vase" of prehistoric art in the United States. Taken from a Moundville, Alabama, site it belongs to the Museum of the American Indian, Heye Foundation in New York City. The high quality of the work indicates that the bowl was probably carved for religious ceremonials. It measures eleven and three-fourth inches in diameter and is made of diorite, a hard greenish stone found in the Far West. No doubt the Moundville Indians acquired this material, as well as many other types of stone and metal, along the well-worn trading paths that linked similar groups over the Americas.

9

(Continued)

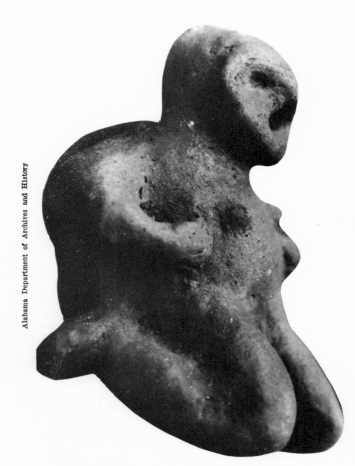

This vessel shows a female figure found with the skeletal remains of a child at Moundville.

Copper Fishhook Used at Moundville in Prehistoric Times

This display in the museum at Mound State Park depicts life as it was when Moundville was the largest city east of the Mississippi river in the days of the Mound Builders. To the right is the Great Temple Mound where religious ceremonies and council meetings took place. The standard rising above the entrance represents the open hand and eye, sacred symbols used by the Moundvillians. To the left a lesser mound is being built as basketfuls of earth are dumped one upon the other.

10

The Moundville potter was a skilled craftsman. The decorations used are strikingly similar to those of the Aztec and Mayan Indians.

One of the strangest customs practiced by the Mound Builders was that of head-flattening. This was done by strapping the head of an infant to a wooden craddleboard with sandbags hanging from either side.

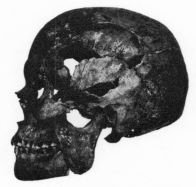

Unflattened Moundville Indian skull

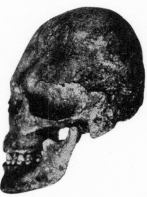

Artificially flattened Moundville Indian skull

This time-phase diorama shows excavation technique used at Moundville. Note the burial made only a few feet under the house.

11

(Continued)

A STONE PENDANT ONCE WORN
BY A MOUNDVILLE INDIAN

One of the fifty-seven skeletons enclosed in the Archeological Museum at Moundville. These skeletons are preserved as they were found.

Dr. Eugene A. Smith, state geologist, purchased this stone disk for one hundred dollars from a Negro plow-hand who turned it up in a field at Moundville. It has since become famous as the "rattlesnake disk." It measures twelve and one-half inches in diameter and was designed to be worn around the neck in religious ceremonials.

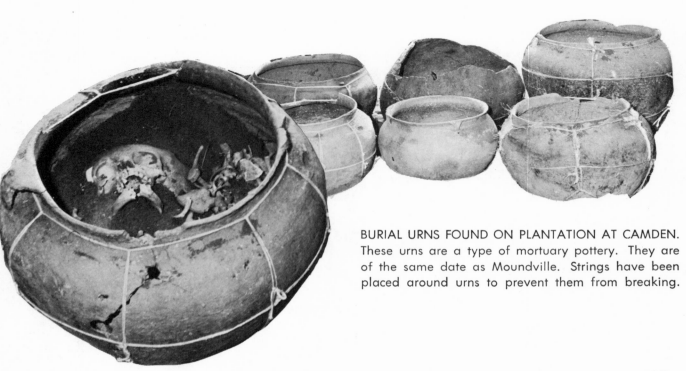

BURIAL URNS FOUND ON PLANTATION AT CAMDEN. These urns are a type of mortuary pottery. They are of the same date as Moundville. Strings have been placed around urns to prevent them from breaking.

13

THE LINGUISTIC STOCK TO WHICH EACH TRIBE
BELONGS IS INDICATED AS FOLLOWS:

MUSKHOGEAN   NO UNDER- OR OVERLINING AND THE
                STOCK IS MADE TO INCLUDE THE
                NATCHEZ AND TIMUCUA GROUPS
                OF LANGUAGES AND THE DOUBT-
                FUL LANGUAGES OF SOUTHERN
                FLORIDA

SIOUAN .... CATAWBA

YUCHEAN .... YUCHI

IROQUOIAN .... CHEROKEE

CADDOAN .... HASINAI

ALGONQUIAN .... POWHATAN

TUNICAN .... TUNICA , INCLUDING THE TUNICA,
                CHITIMACHA AND ATAKAPA
                GROUPS

THE BROKEN LINES INDICATE THE MORE CONTRACT-
ED AND MORE EXPANDED BOUNDARIES OF THE
SOUTHEASTERN CULTURAL PROVINCE

*Location of Indian tribes in the
Southeast about the year 1650*

*A Timucua chief shows a Frenchman how, early each spring, the Indians
offer a stag to the sun and pray for a bountiful harvest of fruits and game.*

First Pictures of Alabama Area Indians

The first encounter in the sixteenth century between the Indians of North America and the European explorers of the New World took place in the southeastern United States. On hand to greet these first white men were Alabama Indians of Muskhogean stock. The Mound Builders had disappeared, probably overrun by these less civilized Muskhogean people, who comprised the largest single Indian group of the same linguistic stock in the Southeast at this time. From them came tribes that later were famous in American history: Creek, Chickasaw, Choctaw, and Seminole. Of the same stock were tribes that later disappeared: Natchez, Timucua, Kosati, Hitchita, and Alabamo. The name Alabama came from this last tribe.

Narratives of these voyages of discovery, sometimes by the explorer himself or members of his expedition, gave the Europeans of the sixteenth and seventeenth century firsthand personal accounts of the Indians. Mapmakers, who frequently were also artists, traveled with these expeditions, and the Indians were fascinating subjects for their drawings. The first Indians which the Europeans knew anything about were the red men of the Southeast.

Explorers found the Indians living in wood or reed houses grouped together around a public square similar to the Moundvillians. Each town or village, as this grouping was called, had its own chief or "micco." This town chief met with a chief speaker who in turn was the head of the entire nation. The towns were widespread but associated closely with all other towns in the tribe.

The natives raised crops of corn, beans, squash, and tobacco in family gardens or on a community plot. Maize or corn figured importantly in their ceremonies. The Green Corn Dance was a yearly affair. As with the Moundville Indians, the religious belief of the tribes centered around the sky or the sun. Some animals were believed to possess magic powers. The priest or medicine men combined magic with healing practices.

Jacques Le Moyne, artist and mapmaker, came with the French Huguenot colony to Florida in 1564 and made the first drawing of Indian life in the United States. This watercolor by Le Moyne shows a tatooed Timucua warrior carrying a powerful bow and a quiver full of poisoned arrows.

Outina, chief of the Timucuas, walks alone in solitary splendor in the middle of his warriors.

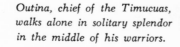

This Indian chief has been doing a bit of trading as evidenced by the coins at his feet. The sunburst disk on his chest is similar to ones found at Moundville. Colorful feathers adorn his headgear and breechcloth.

Marche du Calumet de Paix.

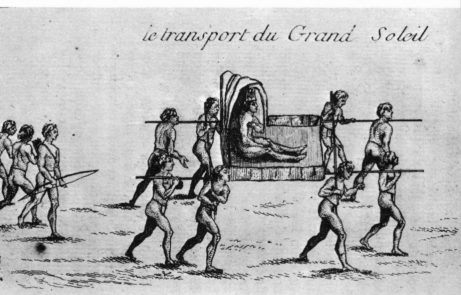

le transport du Grand Soleil

LePage Du Pratz, for his *HISTOIRE DE LA LOUISIANE,* 1758, shows the ceremony of smoking the peace pipe between the Chitimacha Indians and the French. Many such powwows took place around Mobile. Du Pratz came from France to Dauphin Island in 1718 and from there went to live for eight years among the Natchez Indians. The Natchez, like the Mound Builders, were ruled by a king, called the Great Sun, believed to be a descendant of the sun. Here Du Pratz illustrates the manner in which the Great Sun was carried to the harvest festival. In such a manner the Alabama chief Tuscaloosa was borne to greet DeSoto.

16

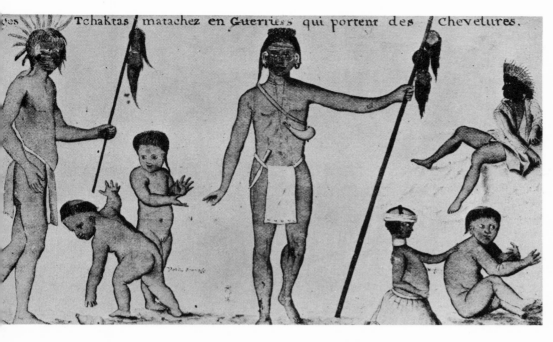

des Tchaktas matachez en Guerriers qui portent des Chevelures.

A French artist, Debatz, painted in 1735 some of the earliest pictures that gave a realistic view of the Indians the first explorers saw. This Debatz' watercolor shows Choctaw Indians of Alabama and Mississippi. The two men are painted for the warpath and carry scalps on poles.

Bernard Roman, Dutch botanist, surveyor, and engraver, came to present Alabama in 1755 and worked for several years recording with his drawings the life of the Indians.

 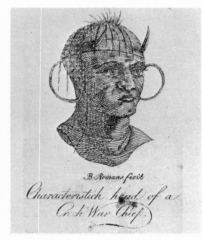

Characteristick Chicasaw head

B Romans fecit
Characteristick head of a Creek War Chief

Choctaw burial ground, drawn by Roman, shows wrapped bodies outside the enclosure. The bones were left until most of the flesh was gone; then they were cleaned by priests and buried in a mound.

Tabula nouarum infularum, quas diuerfis refpectibus Occidentales & Indianas uocant.

Cathay

Quinfay

INDIA fuperior

Hibernia

Archipelagus 7448 infularū

FRANCISCA

C. Britonum

Terra florida

Exteriores

Hispania

Zipangri

Chamaho

Panuco Inf. Tortucarū

Oceanus occidentalis

Medera

Fortunatæ inf.

CVBA

Inf. Hefperidum

AFRICA pars

Antile

Iamica

Dominica

S. Iacobi

PARIAS abundat auro & margaritis

Nouus orbis

Canibali

Sinus Atlanticus

Catigara

Iinfula Atlantica quam uocant Brafilij & Americam.

_pdonum

Die Nüw

Inf. infortu natæ

Welt

Calenfuan

Regio Gigantum

7. infulę Mar gueritarū

Mare pacificum

Fretum Magaliani

Munster's map of the New World appeared in 1540—the same year that De Soto's expedition was making its tedious way in Terra Florida across present Alabama.

COLONIAL ALABAMA

For two hundred years after Columbus discovered America, the exploration of the New World was a geographical feat which rivaled today's space travel. Explorers, seeking gold and glory, ventured across perilous seas, along uncharted coasts, and through unknown interiors. One hundred years before the Pilgrims landed at Plymouth Rock, the southern United States was the testing ground for rivaling monarchs of Europe, and the area which we call Alabama was part of that greatly sought prize. In 1505 a German map made by Martin Waldseemüller showed more about present Alabama and the surrounding area than any other part of North America. In 1519 Pineda entered Mobile Bay, and in 1528 Narvaez wrote of his exploration of the bay. Tristán de Luna commanded one thousand colonists from Veracruz, Mexico, and in 1559 these colonists established a city on Mobile Bay, where they stayed for only two years. Had this colony continued, it would have been the oldest city within the present limits of the United States.

Alabama Bureau of Publicity and Information

The flags of Spain, France, and Great Britain flew over Fort Morgan in Mobile Bay before the American republic was born.

De Soto Explores Alabama

De Soto came to the Alabama area not only to explore but to establish a colony and to rule over it.

The Spanish were the first white men to explore inland from the Gulf and to encounter the Indian tribes of Alabama. While most of the other European countries were split by dissensions in the sixteenth century, Spain prospered at home and abroad and had no rival in her swiftly advancing empire. From Mexico and Peru poured wealth that loaded Spanish ships with the greatest cargoes on earth, and to this Spain wished to add riches from the unexplored areas of Florida, said to contain more gold than Mexico and Peru combined. Spanish Florida of that day extended from the Atlantic coast westward to New Mexico and from the Gulf of Mexico to the North Pole. Spain claimed this vast territory by right of exploration and conquest.

The King of Spain appointed the seasoned conquistador Hernando de Soto to be governor of all Cuba and Florida. Six years previously De Soto had returned from an expedition to Peru wealthier than the king himself, but he now sought this new appointment, expecting to find a country as rich as that of the Aztecs and Incas. If he should also, in the course of his exploration, discover that greatly sought passage to India, for which every explorer since Columbus had looked, so much the better. De Soto spent one year and his entire fortune assembling and equipping an army of select Spanish and Portuguese noblemen. When he sailed to the New World, he was seeking not only gold but the founding of a colony over which he would rule.

(Continued)

This engraving shows De Soto landing at Tampa Bay, Florida, in April 1539. He arrived with the best equipped army of any Spanish explorer to set foot in the New World.

20

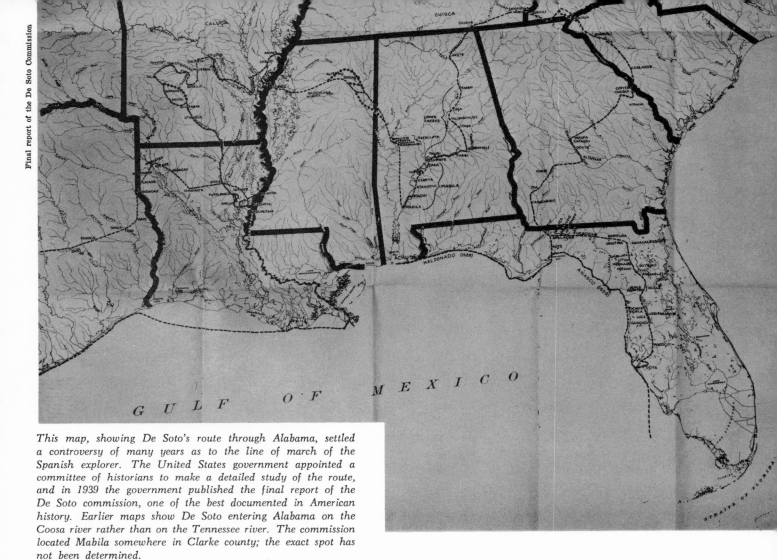

This map, showing De Soto's route through Alabama, settled a controversy of many years as to the line of march of the Spanish explorer. The United States government appointed a committee of historians to make a detailed study of the route, and in 1939 the government published the final report of the De Soto commission, one of the best documented in American history. Earlier maps show De Soto entering Alabama on the Coosa river rather than on the Tennessee river. The commission located Mabila somewhere in Clarke county; the exact spot has not been determined.

In May 1539 De Soto landed at Tampa Bay with the best equipped army of any Spanish explorer to set foot in the New World. Accompanying De Soto was an elaborate invading force: 950 armored soldiers, 200 horses, packs of bloodhounds to run down the Indians, and a herd of hogs that numbered more than a thousand. To convert the savages to Christianity, always an objective of any Spanish expedition, twenty-four priests and monks accompanied the army.

For six months following his landing at Tampa, De Soto explored the state of Florida vainly looking for gold. The Indians, wishing no doubt to be rid of this pillaging and murdering Spaniard, told De Soto of tribes to the north possessing gold. In the spring of 1540 De Soto headed northeast into Georgia. The only treasure he found there was pearls brought from the Atlantic coast by the Indians.

On June 28, 1540, De Soto entered Alabama. For the next five months the Spanish army would make its tedious way over Indian trails across Alabama, pillaging and sometimes killing Indians on the journey. First De Soto crossed the Tennessee river at Burns island into Jackson county. He then traveled from Bridgeport toward Scottsboro, soon crossing the Tennessee river again into the Guntersville area. From there he moved south towards Gadsden and crossed the Coosa river between Gadsden and Talladega. As they traveled De Soto and his men heard rumors of a wealthy Indian town called Coosa, and they headed in this direction.

On July 26 near Childersburg De Soto came upon the most advanced Indian civilization that he was to encounter on his four-year journey. Here were no wild savages such as Europeans visualized but a highly socialized and prosperous people ruled over by a king from his capital city of Coosa. Storehouses overflowed with foods of all kind, but to De Soto's dismay there was no gold. For twenty-five days the Spanish expedition stayed at Coosa, taking food and supplies and making burden bearers of the Indians.

From Coosa the expedition traveled to Tawasa, where Maxwell Air Force Base in Montgomery now stands. Here De Soto heard of gold at Mabila, the largest town of the Gulf coast Indians. From Tawasa he proceeded down the Alabama river to Selma and through Dallas, Wilcox, and Monroe counties to Mabila.

When the Spanish entered the territory of the Mabila tribe, they were met by the giant chief of the Mabilians, Tuscaloosa, borne on a litter by four of his warriors. Covering the litter was a deerskin with a swastika, such as those painted by Moundville Indians. Tuscaloosa seemed unimpressed with the efforts of De Soto's men to awe him with a demonstration of rare horsemanship. Although he finally consented to De Soto's request for

the loan of four hundred Indian carriers, Tuscaloosa gave only evasive response to De Soto's additional request for one hundred Indian women.

All this was too much for the proud Spanish conquistador. As with other Indian chiefs he had already met, De Soto ordered that Tuscaloosa be taken a hostage. He did, however, furnish the chief a horse to ride and allowed him to ride beside him. The attending Indian with the sunshade went along, as well as the Indians carrying pillows for their chief.

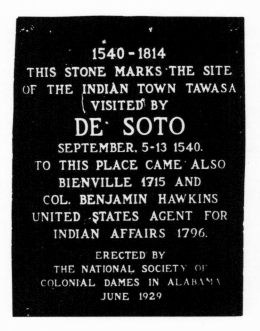

1540 - 1814
THIS STONE MARKS THE SITE OF THE INDIAN TOWN TAWASA VISITED BY
DE SOTO
SEPTEMBER, 5-13 1540.
TO THIS PLACE CAME ALSO BIENVILLE 1715 AND COL. BENJAMIN HAWKINS UNITED STATES AGENT FOR INDIAN AFFAIRS 1796.
ERECTED BY THE NATIONAL SOCIETY OF COLONIAL DAMES IN ALABAMA JUNE 1929

This mural in the state capitol depicts the giant chief of the Mabilians, Tuscaloosa, greeting De Soto.

The Battle of Mabila is portrayed in this miniature display at the Moundville museum. The Indians with clubs, bows, and arrows were no match for the mounted Spanish wielding cross- *bows and swords. In the left foreground an Indian priest entreats the sun god for help while in front of him kneels a Catholic priest.*

The Bloody Battle of Mabila, 1540

On October 18th, 1540, after marching three days with Tuscaloosa as captive, the De Soto expedition reached Mabila. Leaving the army to set up camp outside the walls, De Soto with a group of his captains approached the city, which was enclosed by logs plastered with clay. Tuscaloosa, pretending that he was not a captive, invited them in, and the apparently friendly Indians greeted them with dancing and singing. De Soto and his men dismounted and accompanied Tuscaloosa into the city. As soon as they entered the gates, however, Tuscaloosa disappeared into one of the houses. When an Indian guide refused to obey De Soto's order to bring his chief out, De Soto's captain, Baltasar de Gallegos, killed the guide with his lance. Immediately many Indians poured out of houses and the battle began.

The Spaniards tried to reach the gate on foot, not having time to mount their horses. De Soto ran, falling several times in his attempt to get to the gate. The Indians tried to prevent the Spaniards from escaping by closing the gate, but De Soto and most of his men managed to get through. Outside the gate De Soto rallied his men and withdrew some distance from the city with the Indians in pursuit. After three hours of fighting the Indians retreated into the stockaded city. De Soto's men stormed the gates and broke through some of the walls with their axes.

In one last desperate effort the Indians, including women and children, fought in the open square, from the housetops, and from the walls. After rescuing a group of Spaniards trapped in one of the houses, De Soto ordered his men to set fire to the city. Escape for the Indians was impossible, and many of them threw themselves into the fire preferring death to captivity.

This memorable fight lasted all day and ended at sunset with a Spanish victory. There were twenty Spaniards dead and scores wounded with only one physician to treat them. Soldiers themselves used the fat taken from the bodies of the dead Indians to treat their wounds, a method that some had learned in Peru. Many of their horses had been killed. They lost much of their clothing, the vessels used in celebrating mass, their supply of gunpowder, and the only treasure they had found so far—the pearls. Estimates of the Indian dead by De Soto's captains present that day range from 2,500 to 11,000. The battle of Mabila cost more lives than any one-day battle ever fought between white men and Indians on North American soil.

De Soto rested for twenty-eight days after the battle of Mabila and then, still seeking gold, he resumed his march westward across the Warrior and Tombigbee rivers into Mississippi even though his ship waited in Mobile Bay. The well-equipped expedition which had entered Alabama hopefully in July left the state in November, battle weary and mutinous.

At the age of forty-two De Soto died and was buried in the Mississippi river, his dreams of gold buried with him. But the Spanish cause was not yet lost. Spanish galleons, sailing home along the Gulf coast through the Caribbean and West Indies, carried back treasures from the New World. For a time the French, English, and Dutch were content to rob richly-laden Spanish ships, but soon they too came to plunder the New World. Spain realized too late that her enemies were gaining a permanent foothold. After the defeat of the Spanish Armada in 1588, Spain was no longer able to defend her Gulf coast possessions.

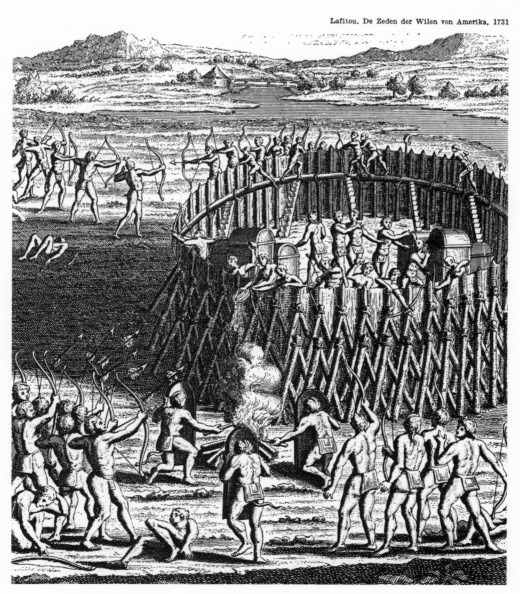

Lafitou, De Zeden der Wilen von Amerika, 1731

The smaller Indian villages which De Soto visited as he marched through Alabama were probably like the one pictured here in this old print.

CARTE DE LA LOUISIANE ET DU COURS DU MISSISSIPI *Dressée sur un grand nombre de Mémoires entr'autres sur ceux de M. le Maire Par Guill. Delisle de l'Academie R. des Scien.*

Delisle's 1718 map of the Louisiana Province shows the Mobile area in detail.

Louis XIV

The Louisiana Province was named for Louis XIV. This portrait painted by Maltby Sykes hangs in the French room of the Alabama Department of Archives and History.

D'Iberville

Louis XIV chose d'Iberville, colorful Canadian naval hero, to locate a site for the French capital on the Gulf coast. D'Iberville became the first governor of the Louisiana Province and founder of Fort Louis at Twenty-seven Mile Bluff.

Fort Louis de la Mobile

After the Spanish the French were the next Europeans to enter the Alabama area. France had established a fur trading empire in Canada and now sought to expand "New France" to the Gulf coast. In 1682 the French explorer, Robert Cavelier de la Salle, making his way southward from Canada, erected a cross at the mouth of the Mississippi river. Then with drawn sword LaSalle claimed Louisiana in the name of the French king, Louis XIV. Louis selected the colorful Canadian naval hero, Pierre le Moyne, Sieur d'Iberville, to explore the Gulf coast, select a capital site, and colonize it. D'Iberville placed his nineteen-year-old brother, Bienville, second in command. In 1699 the French brothers, probing eastward along the Gulf coast looking for a likely harbor, sailed into Mobile Bay with their fleet. Exploring an island a few miles out in the bay from the present city of Mobile, they saw what appeared to be a "natural mountain of bones." On closer inspection they found it to be the skeletal remains of Indians. It was obvious from the bones that the Indians had been beheaded. The Frenchmen called the spot Massacre Island, and later changed the name to Dauphin Island. From that time on Dauphin Island served as the port of entry for the Louisiana colony.

From Mobile Bay the le Moyne brothers explored up the winding Mobile river, seeking a high and protected spot to build the capital city. As the site for their capital they chose a cliff at present Twenty-Seven Mile Bluff. With the Fleur de Lis waving overhead, the Frenchmen knelt under the pines and asked for a divine blessing on this chosen spot. Yet Fort Louis was only a temporary halt in French explorations that would a few years later lead to the founding of Mobile.

Using Fort Louis as a base, the le Moyne brothers explored the Gulf coast, establishing colonies at Biloxi and New Orleans. Then d'Iberville returned to France for reinforcements and supplies, leaving Bienville to govern the colonies. To make the colonization more permanent, d'Iberville persuaded twenty-three girls to come from France as brides. In 1704 the girls arrived at Fort Louis carrying their possessions in small trunks or cassettes. They became known as the "cassette girls."

In 1706, without having established a permanent site in the Alabama area, d'Iberville died from yellow fever. The saddened and lonely young Governor Bienville found himself left with various problems. Although some of the colonists were of hardy stock from the Canadian woods, few were trained farmers. Food shortage, Indian disturbances, floods, and fever plagued the new settlement. In 1711 Bienville abandoned the site of Twenty-Seven Mile Bluff and relocated Fort Louis at Mobile. The French at last had established their permanent city in the southern part of present Alabama.

With patience and wisdom Bienville for many years served the city he had founded. He was a colonizer rather than a seeker of New World silver or gold. He foresaw the productive potential of the new province and was responsible for initiating the plantation idea that later flourished. Bienville introduced the first cattle, hogs, and chickens. He grew and shipped the first cotton and tobacco, and he experimented with the raising of indigo and silk. He gave Mobile its first camellias and azaleas imported from France.

When, in 1722, Louis XIV granted the Louisiana colony to a company founded by Crozat, the company replaced Bienville with Cadillac as governor. Cadillac, however, proved incapable of dealing with all the growing pains of the colonies. In 1733 the company persuaded Bienville to return to the colony as its governor. In 1743 he voluntarily retired and spent his last years in Paris.

FOUNDING OF MOBILE, 1711, BY BIENVILLE

Mural by Roderick MacKenzie, State Capitol, Montgomery

Madam Octavia LeVert, prominent literary and social figure, maintained in Mobile a salon famous for its conversation and its shaping of political affairs not only in Alabama but in the nation. This portrait hangs in the Alabama Department of Archives and History.

This panoramic sketch of Mobile shows many architectural styles. In the foreground is the city hall with its cupola suggesting Spanish influence. At left is the Mobile county courthouse with its classic French architecture. Across from the city hall is the French colonial home of Madam LeVert.

Spain

France

Great Britain

Confederate States of America

United States of A

UNDER FIVE FLAGS

The French flag was the first of five flags to wave over Mobile. Eventually Spain, Britain, the Confederate States of America, and the United States occupied this important port city. These various influences gave Mobile a gracious cosmopolitan flavor, enhancing its cultural and social life, and greatly influencing its architecture and customs.

Many times the flag over Mobile was not that over the rest of Alabama. In 1798 the present states of Mississippi and Alabama became the Mississippi Territory except for Mobile. In 1780 the Spanish governor, Galvez, captured Mobile and controlled it for the next twenty-one years. In 1800 Napoleon forced Spain to cede the prov-

ince of Louisiana to France, and in 1803 President Jefferson purchased Louisiana from France. The boundaries were not clear, however, and Mobile remained Spanish until 1813, when General Wilkinson, using the War of 1812 as the pretext, ousted the Spanish commandant and seized Mobile for the United States.

Always a center of activity, Mobile prospered under American rule. The United States granted Mobile a town charter in 1814. River steamers brought cotton down the Tombigbee and the Alabama rivers to this, the only port city in the state. Planters with profits from the year's crops arrived for festivities and spent their money freely.

MOBILE
Port city with
Old World charm

From this carriage block on Government street full-skirted ladies in antebellum days stepped into carriages with relative ease.

The atmosphere of the West Indies clings to this delicate French colonial building, which was originally a market and then a city hall.

Here at the turn of the twentieth century is a toll house on the Bay Shell Road outside Mobile.

Bienville Square, named for the founder of the city, is the most picturesque spot in downtown Mobile.

The Sand Island lighthouse at the mouth of Mobile Bay is a well-known landmark. Large stones at the base are said to be ballast from old sailing vessels.

Besides Dauphin street, pictured here in 1901, other prominent Mobile streets with French names include Royal, Conti, St. Charles, and Conception.

31

(Continued)

In spite of damage from hurricanes Christ Episcopal church stands today, a fine example of Greek Doric architecture. Ten thousand Mexican silver pesos went into its altar cross.

Lacy iron grillwork — the hallmark of Mobile

The blessing of the shrimp fleet at Bayou La Batre dates back to the French.

The first Mardi Gras celebration in the New World was held in Mobile. Colorful parades and balls still enliven the city during the week before Lent.

Buried in this old cemetery are many of the city's first residents. Most graves are above ground to avoid water damage.

Photo by Victor Haagen

(Continued)

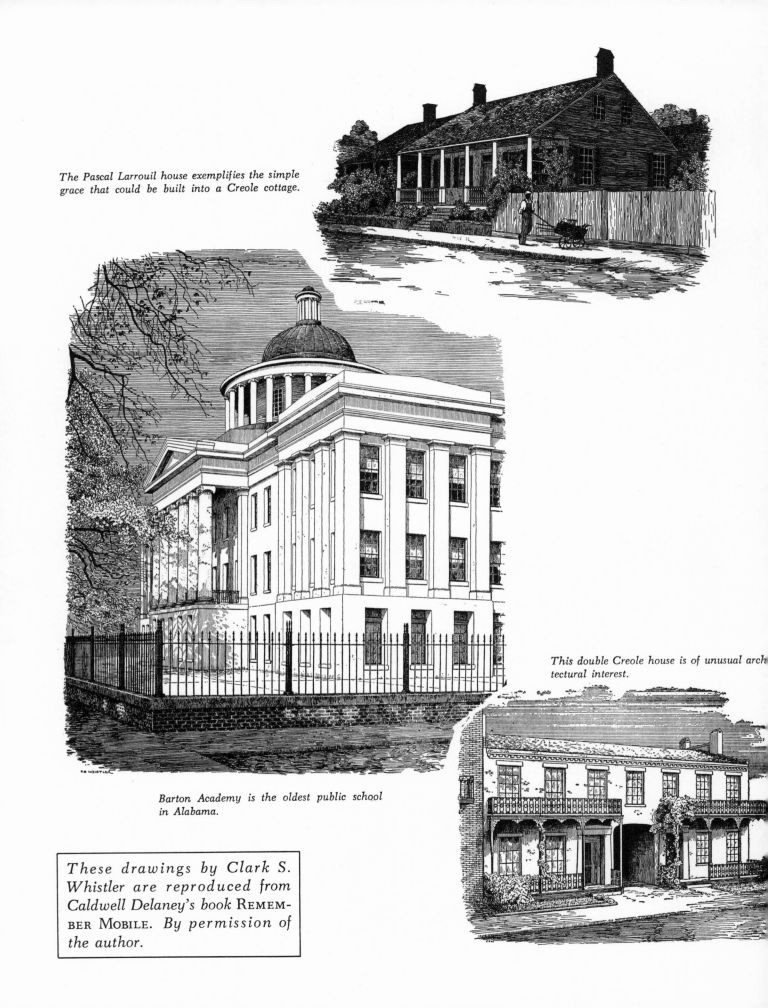

The Pascal Larrouil house exemplifies the simple grace that could be built into a Creole cottage.

This double Creole house is of unusual architectural interest.

Barton Academy is the oldest public school in Alabama.

These drawings by Clark S. Whistler are reproduced from Caldwell Delaney's book REMEMBER MOBILE. By permission of the author.

Spring Hill College, a Jesuit school founded
in 1830, attracted from its beginning students
from Europe and Latin America.

At her Georgia cottage in Spring Hill, Augusta
Evans Wilson wrote ST. ELMO and VASHTI.

As far as is known the Durand house, built in
1796, is the only eighteenth century building
remaining in Mobile.

First American Settlers in Alabama

While the French sought the Gulf area during the eighteenth century, the English and Dutch and sometimes the Spanish were busy on the Atlantic coast but with their gaze always westward. Twenty-two years after the French founded Mobile, the English established their thirteenth colony, Georgia. Next in their path westward was Alabama, still part of the Louisiana Territory. To stop this westward English thrust, the French in 1714 built Fort Toulouse where the Coosa and Tallapoosa rivers join and Fort Tombeckbe on the Tombigbee river. By 1763, however, at the close of the French Indian War the British inherited Alabama and ruled until the end of the American Revolution.

The Revolutionary War was not a small brush war consisting of thirteen colonies fighting only in the Americas. It was a world war fought on the high seas as well as in many colonies. Territories changed from British to French to Spanish and back again. This was nowhere more true than in Alabama.

Bernardo Galvez, governor of Spanish Louisiana, captured Mobile in 1780 and claimed all the area east of the Mississippi river as part of his empire. Shortly after George Washington became president of the United States, Galvez's successor, Estevan Miro, built St. Steph-

ens on the Tombigbee river. It was another link in the chain of forts constructed to hold back the eager homesteading Americans already spilling into the Mississippi Territory. When the Americans established the Mississippi Territory in 1798, it was a blow to the Spanish that St. Stephens was on the American side of the Ellicott Line.

While the countries of Spain and France failed to gain firm footholds in the Alabama area, English-speaking pioneers were penetrating the wilderness with increasing determination. Most of these pioneers migrated southwestward from the original thirteen English colonies, including many from Georgia and South Carolina. However, there was a fourteenth English colony that was also important. Much of this colony was in Alabama as part of what was then called West Florida. From the eastern part of West Florida came pioneers seeking Indian trade or Indian land or perhaps adventure in the remote Indian country.

These earliest pioneers were usually English; however, there were Spaniards, Frenchmen, Scotsmen, Dutchmen, and Germans. A surprising number of the earliest Alabama pioneers were originally Scotch traders who won respect among the Indians, later married into

(Continued)

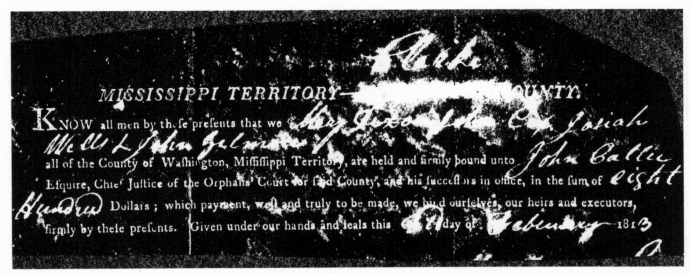

Clarke County Deed Book File

This mural from the state capitol depicts the famed frontiersman, Sam Dale, known as Big Sam, leading a wagon train into present Alabama. In 1793 at the age of twenty-one Dale helped cut a wagon road into the Mississippi Territory from Georgia. Later he made a wagon trail through the Cherokee nation to the Mississippi river and established trading posts along the way. At the beginning of the Creek Indian War Dale learned from his Indian friends that the Creeks were getting guns, powder, and lead from the Spanish in Pensacola and warned the whites that the Indians were planning to attack the settlers.

an influential family in the tribe, and became wealthy and respected leaders. Famous offsprings of such marriages included William Weatherford, Alexander Mc-Gillivray, Menawa, and William Colbert. These half-breeds were a valuable go-between, understanding both the Indian's and white man's way of life.

The first English-speaking settlement in Alabama was the Tombigbee-Tensaw community, founded in the middle of the eighteenth century. Pioneers in this Tombigbee area organized a trading post near Tensaw, in present Baldwin county. In this area arose some of our state's first large plantations. During the American Revolution a number of Tory refugees from the Carolinas and Georgia settled here. Near the turn of the twentieth century Alabama historian A. B. Meek wrote that these Tory refugees "laid the first foundations of American inheritance in the counties of Clarke, Washington, and Baldwin." Sometimes pioneers from this area traveled to Natchez, capital of the Mississippi Territory, the nearest town for conducting important legal affairs.

Such hardy pioneers put together crude log cabins with Spanish moss and clay. They built sawmills and brickyards, and they floated lumber down the river to Mobile to be shipped to the West Indies. The rich black soil produced fine cotton, which was ginned at the Boat Yard on the Tensaw river. At the Boat Yard, John and William Pierce, operators of the gin, founded Alabama's first known school in 1799.

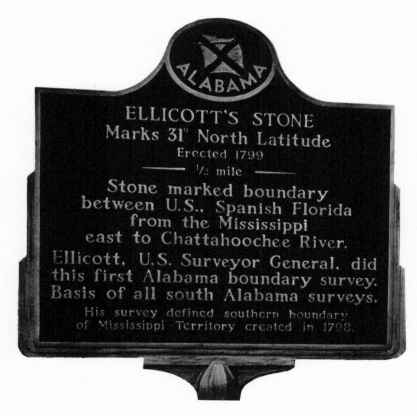

Marker on U. S. 43 north of Mobile

Surveyors worked diligently to mark the Ellicott line across the Alabama countryside. To perform this work Spain chose Sir William Dunbar, a British subject, and the United States chose Andrew Ellicott of Maryland. These two men worked together on the project, beginning at opposite ends. They had trouble with the Indians stealing supplies and helpers refusing to work under difficult conditions. It took the surveyors three years to establish the boundary to everyone's satisfaction. Because St. Stephens was almost on the line, the Spaniards thought the valuable fort would fall to them. The Spanish, however, respected their agreement, and on May 5, 1799, the two nations flew appropriate flags over their new areas.

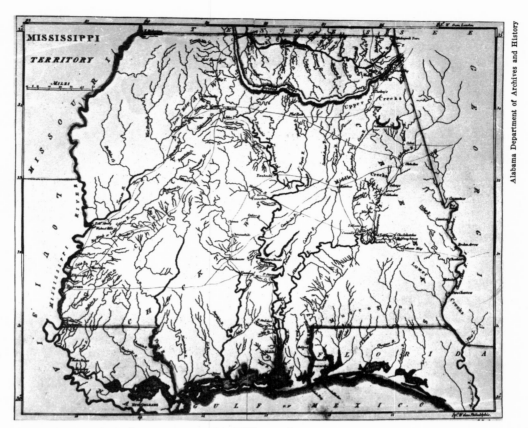

Alabama Department of Archives and History

The predominantly Indian names on this 1817 map by John Melish leave no doubt that the American pioneers had made little impact on the Mississippi Territory.

Library of Congress

...ndian raid on a pioneer settlement. The Indians considered the Mississippi Territory part of their ancestral land, and the white man an invader.

Kendall, Life of Andrew Jackson

In 1807 Aaron Burr, charged with treason by the United States, fled from Natchez to seek refuge with Colonel John Hinson in Alabama's Tombigbee-Tensaw area. Nicholas Perkins, a lawyer, recognized Burr as the man pictured here and summoned Captain Edmund Pendleton Gaines, commanding officer at nearby Fort Stoddard, to arrest the former vice-president. Perkins then headed a group of eight men selected to return Burr to United States authorities in Richmond.

The Red Man Learns the White Man's Ways

Moore, History of Alabama

George Strothers Gaines became an Indian agent to the Choctaws in 1800 with headquarters at St. Stephens. He had great influence upon the Choctaws and was a trusted friend of Chief Pushmataha.

At the time that Alabama was being settled by white men, the largest Indian population of the Southeast was concentrated within its borders. Cherokees lived in the farthest northeastern area; Chickasaws, in the northwestern; Choctaws, in the southwest; and Creeks, who far outnumbered all others, on the Coosa and Tallapoosa rivers.

To the Indians, caught on their own land between powerful enemies, it became necessary to serve whatever master offered the best chance of survival. It was to these same Indians that the first colonists had turned to learn how to survive in the new country. The Indians taught them how to blaze a trail, how to build a fire and how to signal with smoke, how to hunt deer and other game, how to trap and how to dress the skins. From the Indians the white man learned how to make a canoe, and how to use it on the waterways that were the highways of Alabama.

As time went by, however, the Indians became increasingly dependent upon the European settlers instead of the settlers upon them. The Indians' way of life had been weakened by the depletion of wild game, disabling epidemics of disease, too much rum, and their attraction for European goods such as bells, mirrors, knives, and glass bottles.

The Indian chiefs visited the white men's main settlements and dealt with their governors and councilors. Some of the Alabama area Indians, particularly the Cherokees and Creeks who were allies of the British, traveled to England on official business. Since the voyages of Columbus, the Indians of America had held a strange fascination for Europeans. Europeans knew of them through the tales and the drawings of the early explorations of the New World. From the sixteenth century to the nineteenth, tales of the "noble savage" were commonplace in Europe. Europeans visualized the Indian as an ideal man, simple and virtuous, living in a Utopian world.

In London delegations of Creeks and Cherokees created excitement not only among the nobility by whom they were received but among ordinary Londoners. A favorite pastime of the Indians was having their portraits painted. Sir Joshua Reynolds and Francis Parsons painted groups of the visiting Indians, whose dress, combining European styles with feathers and scalp locks, had become gradually more like the white man's. When Oliver Goldsmith met a delegation of Cherokees, he presented a present to their chief and in return received a kiss. He complained of the vermillion stain which the Indian left on his face.

With the signing of the Louisiana Purchase Treaty, Americans began to move into the newly opened lands in unprecedented numbers. To protect themselves the Creeks formed a confederation, centered along the Coosa, Tallapoosa, Alabama, and Chattahoochee rivers, and divided themselves into the Upper and Lower Creeks. Here the European powers in the nineteenth century played out the contest for possession of the New World.

Near Wetumpka, Alabama, in the heart of the Creek nation resided the undisputed leader of this powerful confederation, Alexander McGillivray, often called the "Tallyrand of Alabama." Around McGillivray centered the rivalry of three nations for the control of Indian lands. First he championed the British cause, promising them the Creeks' support against the Americans. After the Americans defeated the British, McGillivray accepted money from both the Spanish and the Americans, promising each country his support against the other. McGillivray obtained the rank of brigadier general in the United States Army and of colonel in the Spanish Army. He delighted in parading in his uniforms before his Creek admirers at Little Tallassee. McGillivray's influence came to an end when both the Americans and the Spaniards discovered his intrigues. In 1793 he died in Pensacola, Florida, disowned by the three countries whose uniforms he had in turn worn so proudly.

Even though the Indians considered the white man an intruder, they imitated many of his ways to improve their own way of life. Indians purchased cattle, slaves, firearms, and ploughs. Even their houses and clothes began to resemble those of their neighbors. The Indians were trying hard to become "civilized," and had it not been for conflicting ideas of landownership it is possible that the Indians and the white settlers could have found a peaceful co-existence. Their mutual desire for landownership led to bitterness and to the Creek Indian War.

Massachusetts Historical Society

a Bureau of Publicity and Information

I Alexander McGillivray, Agent to the Creek nation of Indians, and Brigadier General in the service of the United States, do solemnly swear to bear true allegiance to the said United States of America, And to serve them honestly and faithfully against all their enemies or opposers whomsoever, and to observe and Obey the orders of the President of the United States of America. And the Orders of the officers appointed over me, According to the articles of war, and the true intent and meaning of the Secret articles of the treaty of peace, made and concluded between the united States of America, and the Creek nation of Indians. On the seventh day of the Present month of August.

Alex: McGillivray

Sworn before me in the City of New York This Fourteenth day of August in the year of our Lord One thousand Seven hundred and Ninety.

John Blair an associate judge of the supreme Court of the United States

McGillivray's oath of allegiance to the United States. In 1790 McGillivray went to New York to discuss land cessions with George Washington.

Chief Calvin McGhee, modern Creek Indian of Alabama, surveys a collection of Indian trade beads in the Alabama Department of Archives and History. For centuries the Indians used these beads, called wampum, for trading purposes. Many beads could be strung on a necklace or belt and conveniently carried over long distances.

Smithsonian Institution, Bureau of American Ethnology

This sketch made in 1791 shows Creek Indians living in a log cabin in much the same manner as their white neighbors.

41

(Continued)

This dance preceded the ball game. The warriors carried eagle tail feathers, and their bodies were painted white. This same ceremony with the same costumes was probably being performed when the first white man came to Alabama.

The ball is up and the game is underway. Players were often seriously injured or killed in their attempt to get the hard deerskin ball from each other. The long rackets were used to hit not only the ball but other players as well.

In 1834 at Fort Gibson, Oklahoma, George Catlin, foremost Indian artist, painted these scenes of Choctaws playing their traditional ball game, which they had brought from Alabama and Mississippi.

efore the game starts the warriors dance around the goal posts hile the squaws perform on the playing field.

CHOCTAW BALL PLAYER

Play ball, somewhat similar to modern lacrosse, was a favorite game of the Indians. Tribes sometimes played this game to settle disputes.

THE CREEK INDIAN WAR

By 1812 the Creeks, who far outnumbered all other tribes in Alabama, were ready to fight. They were frustrated by the failure of many treaties with the "Great White Father" in Washington who had promised to protect their lands. Available to them were arms supplied by British agents from Spanish-held Mobile. The British, already engaged in the War of 1812 with the United States, were anxious to have the Indians as an ally, and the Spanish encouraged the British as Spain still claimed that the Mobile area was not part of the Louisiana Purchase. The resulting conflict became known as the Creek Indian War.

The Creeks were influenced by the Shawnee Chief Tecumseh, himself baited by the British, who tried to persuade all Indian tribes in the United States to protect themselves against the American frontiersmen. On this mission, Tecumseh came to Alabama, accompanied by the famous Shawnee medicine man, Sukabo, who was born in Alabama near Tuskegee. Traveling on black ponies, Tecumseh's party visited the Chickasaws, the Choctaws, and the Creeks.

On his Alabama visit, Sukabo made a prophet of one of the most famous and powerful Indians in the Creek Indian War, Josiah Francis (Hillis Hadjo). Francis in turn created among the Creeks many prophets who came to control the anti-American faction and were responsible for the direction of the war.

The Creeks were the only tribe in Alabama to support Tecumseh even though some of their chiefs refused to fight against the United States. The warriors voted by throwing their tomahawks either to the white or red side of the council fire. Those favoring war became the Red Sticks; the others became the White Sticks.

Scattered skirmishes between Creek Indians and settlers opened the bloody Creek Indian War in Alabama. The first action was around the Bigbee settlement at Burnt Corn creek, where an unjust attack had been made upon a group of Creek half-bloods returning from Pensacola with war supplies. Word spread among the Indians, and they prepared for full scale war. Nearby settlers became alarmed and fled to Fort Mims for protection.

When Tecumseh came to Alabama in 1811 to unite the Choctaws and Creeks with the Indian tribes of the Northeast, he brought with him the well-known prophet and medicine man Sukabo, who was born in Alabama. This old engraving depicts Sukabo striving to endow a follower with prophetic powers by the laying on of hands.

Benjamin Hawkins, Indian agent to the Alabama tribes for more than twenty-five years, attached so little importance to Tecumseh's visit that he left Tuckabatchee several weeks before he knew Tecumseh would address the Creek National Council. Hawkins had tried for many years to Americanize the Indian way of life with better agricultural methods and with new industries while Tecumseh had urged his people to retain their land and old customs.

THIS STONE PLACED AT THE
GREAT COUNCIL TREE
MARKS THE SITE OF
TUKABAHCHI
1686-1836
CAPITAL OF THE UPPER CREEK INDIAN
NATION. HERE WERE BORN EFAU HAUJO,
GREAT MEDAL CHIEF, AND OPOTHLEYAHOLO,
CREEK LEADERS. BIG WARRIOR RESIDED
NEARBY. HERE CAME TECUMSEH IN 1811
TO AROUSE THE NATIVES AGAINST THE
WHITE SETTLERS AND WAS SUCCESSFULLY
OPPOSED BY COL. BENJAMIN HAWKINS,
PRINCIPAL AGENT FOR INDIAN AFFAIRS
SOUTH OF THE OHIO RIVER. HERE IN 1823
LEE COMPERE ESTABLISHED A BAPTIST
MISSION SCHOOL.

PLACED MAY 13, 1929
BY THE ALABAMA
ANTHROPOLOGICAL SOCIETY

Both: Smithsonian Institution, Bureau of American Ethnology

Menawa

THE INDIAN LEADERS

Bitter enemy of William McIntosh and the Americans was Menawa, war chief of the Creek nation in the Creek Indian War. He labeled McIntosh a traitor to his people and helped to plan his execution. When Tecumseh visited the Creeks in 1811, Menawa fell under his influence and used his power to organize the Upper Creeks against the Americans. Menawa fought in several battles during the war and is best known for his leadership in the Battle of Horseshoe Bend.

Pushmataha

The role of mediator fell to the Choctaw chief, Pushmataha, in the early stages of the Creek Indian War. He matched his oratory with Tecumseh and influenced his own tribe, as well as the Chickasaws, to fight with the Americans against the Creeks and their British ally. The United States rewarded him with a commission as general in the army, and he is shown here wearing the epaulets of his rank.

Pushmataha died in Washington, D. C., in 1824 while on a mission from the Choctaw nation. On his deathbed he requested that he be given a military funeral. "Let the big guns be fired over me," he said. "When you shall come to your home, they will ask you, 'Where is Pushmataha?' and you will say to them, 'He is no more.' They will hear the tidings like the sound of the fall of a mighty oak in the stillness of the woods." The United States buried Pushmataha with full military honors in the Congressional National Cemetery in Washington, D. C.

William McIntosh

Strongest Indian ally of the Americans during the Creek Indian War was William McIntosh, who headed a minority group of Creeks favoring the White Sticks or peace group. His father had been a captain in the British army, and his mother was a full-blooded Creek. Soon after the war started, McIntosh sent a band of warriors to Tuckabatchee to fight the Upper Creeks who were rebelling against the Americans. McIntosh fought at the Battle of Atossee opposing the Red Sticks and so distinguished himself that General John Floyd cited him for bravery. At the Battle of Horseshoe Bend he commanded Indian forces, and General Jackson called him Major McIntosh. McIntosh was one of the signers of the treaty of Fort Jackson, August 9, 1814, which ended the Creek Indian War. In the Seminole War, McIntosh headed a group of Creek warriors serving with General Jackson in Florida. He was commissioned a general and placed in charge of all Indian troops in that territory.

After the Seminole War McIntosh returned to Georgia and became a wealthy cotton planter, owning many Negro slaves. In 1825 he signed the Treaty of Indian Springs, which ceded most of the remaining Creek lands to the United States. Because he had signed this treaty without the consent of his people, a secret council of the Upper Creeks sent 175 warriors to dispose of McIntosh on his Georgia plantation. They set fire to the house and killed McIntosh as he fled from the burning building. Both the Creeks and the Cherokees had passed laws establishing the death penalty for making such cessions.

This life-sized portrait of William McIntosh, painted by Washington Allston, hangs in the Alabama Department of Archives and History. Peter A. Brannon, former director of the department, discovered the portrait in a bar in Columbus, Georgia, in 1900. According to Brannon the painting was given by Chilly McIntosh, a son of William McIntosh, in payment of a debt, and the picture was eventually hung in the bar where Brannon found it.

Alabama Department of Archives and History

*This marker is beside Alabama
Highway 59 in Baldwin county.*

DRAWING OF FORT MIMS,

Found among Gen Claiborne's manuscript papers.

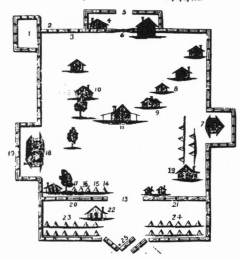

*This plan of Fort Mims was found among
the manuscripts of General F. L. Claiborne
and was first published in Pickett's HIS-
TORY OF ALABAMA.*

Fort Mims Massacre

Fort Mims, twenty miles north of Mobile, was typical of
fortifications that the Alabama settlers erected against possibility
of surprise Indian attacks upon their homes. The settlers usually
built such fortifications around the largest farmhouse in the
area. With their women and children safe in the fort, sometimes
the men were able to continue the farm work during the day.
Since such fortifications often gave a false sense of security, the
settlers attempted to live life as usual although surrounded by
hostile Indians. Knowing this, the Indians planned a surprise
attack on Fort Mims when the settlers were assembled for their
midday meal.

On August 30, 1813, a thousand warriors under William
Weatherford and the leading prophet, Josiah Francis, fell upon
Fort Mims. They slipped into the eastern gate, which had been
carelessly left open and was loosely guarded. Within a short time
the Creek warriors had scalped and burned 517 men, women,
and children—one of the bloodiest massacres in American history. The conflict had now changed from a civil war to a war
against the United States.

48

From the Mobile Register.

The Canoe Battle.

PLANTATION, May 5, 1860.

Dear Sir: I have been often requested to point out the place where the canoe battle was fought. I have therefore, on the first day of this month, placed a sign board upon a cedar post at the point where we were surrounded, and from whence we embarked to made the attack. It will be found on the east bank, 40 feet above Mr. George Foster's landing.—Please give notice of the same.

Your obedient servant,

J. AUSTILL.

The Canoe Fight

One of the favorite stories in Alabama history concerns the canoe fight in which three frontiersmen and a Negro named Caesar defeated eleven Indians. The incident occurred when a group of settlers went out to look for Indian war parties. Captain Sam Dale with eighty volunteers was pursuing the redskins in the canebrakes when this most famous single-handed exploit of the Creek Indian War took place.

On the morning of November 20, 1813, Sam Dale's scouting party saw a large canoe containing eleven Creek warriors floating down the Alabama river near Randon's creek in Monroe county. Captain Dale and two soldiers, Jeremiah Austill and James Smith, accompanied by Caesar, pushed out into the Alabama river to challenge the Indians. Albert Pickett, in his *History of Alabama,* published in 1851, wrote from first-hand accounts this colorful description of the incident:

"The noble Caesar paddled towards the Indian's canoe, and, when within twenty yards of it, the three resolute Americans rose to give them a broadside; but only the gun of Smith fired. Caesar was ordered to paddle up, and to place his boat side by side with that of the warriors. Approaching within ten feet, the Chief, recognizing Dale, exclaimed, 'Now for it, Big Sam!' At the same instant, he presented his gun at Austill's breast. That brave youth struck at him with an oar, which he dodged, and in return he brought down his rifle upon Austill's head, just as the canoes came together. At that moment, the powerful arms of Smith and Dale raised their long rifles, which came down with deadly force, and felled the Chief to the bottom of the canoe—his blood and brains bespattering its sides. Such was the force of the blow inflicted by Dale, that his gun was broken near the lock. Seizing the heavy barrel, still left, he did great execution with it to the end of the combat. Austill, in a moment, engaged with the second warrior, and then with a third, both of whom he dispatched with his clubbed rifle. Smith, too, was equally active, having knocked down two Indians. Caesar had by this time got the canoes close together, and held them with a mighty grasp, which enabled Dale, who was in the advance, and the others to maintain a firm footing by keeping their feet in both canoes. These brave men now mowed down the savages, amid the encouraging shouts of the men on both sides of the river, who had a full view of the deadly conflict . . . Having laid all the warriors low, these undaunted Americans began to cast them into the bright waters of the Alabama, their native stream, now to be their grave. Every time a savage was raised up from the bottom of the canoe by the head and heels and slung into the water, the Americans upon the banks sent up lengthy shouts, as some slight revenge for the tragedy of Fort Mims."

"Remember Fort Mims"

"Remember Fort Mims" became a rallying cry on the frontier around the Creek country. Militia from Georgia and the Mississippi Territory moved against the Indians, but it was the two thousand volunteers from Tennessee under Andrew Jackson that spelled doom for the Creeks.

When George S. Gaines, Indian agent at St. Stephens, heard of the Indian attack on Fort Mims, he sent word to Andrew Jackson for help. Jackson, wounded from a fight, lay in his bed at the Hermitage in Nashville, but in response to Gaines' request he sent Colonel John Coffee ahead to scout the Indian country with his mounted troops. Nine days after dispatching Colonel Coffee, a weak and pale General Jackson moved south with his volunteer Tennessee militia to join the colonel. The army hacked its way through the dense forests making trails that later became the roads the first settlers followed into Alabama. Passing present day Huntsville, Jackson erected defenses on the Tennessee river at Fort Deposit. When he heard that the Creek village of Tallushatchee close by had only about two hundred of Weatherford's warriors defending it, Jackson sent Coffee with one thousand men against the village. Present that day was young Davy Crockett, already an experienced Indian scout, who later wrote of the fight: "We shot them like dogs."

With Coffee attacking the Indian village, Jackson took his main army and crossed Sand Mountain. When he came to the Coosa river at Ten Islands, he erected a base called Fort Strother.

In the meantime, Weatherford had assembled about one thousand Creek warriors to move against some of his own people who lived in a village called Talladega and were refusing to prepare battle against the whites. Weatherford felt that this village should be punished because of its disloyalty to the Creek nation in refusing to fight. General Jackson, on the other hand, felt that these people should be protected against Weatherford. From a friendly warrior who had escaped from Talladega through Weatherford's camp, Jackson learned of Weatherford's impending attack. The Indian had covered himself with the skin of a hog and, grunting and rooting in a crawling position, had escaped and made his way to Fort Strother. Jackson won the battle of Talladega and lost only fifteen men. For Weatherford, however, the loss was great; three hundred dead warriors lay scattered on the battlefield.

Militiamen raid a Creek village on the Tallapoosa river.

From an old print

This portrait of Andrew Jackson hangs in the Alabama Department of Archives and History. It was copied by Alabama artist Maltby Sykes from a Thomas Sully portrait in the Cochran Gallery, Washington, D. C.

General Andrew Jackson

Governor William Blount

General John Coffee

General John Coffee, brother-in-law of Andrew Jackson, was in command of the mounted Tennessee volunteers. He served under Jackson at the Battle of Horseshoe Bend and in many other engagements. After the Creek Indian War Coffee became a surveyor for the Mississippi Territory. He settled in north Alabama and was one of the first landholders in the Tennessee valley. This picture is from a miniature at the Hermitage in Nashville.

Governor William Blount of Tennessee was most sympathetic to the call for help from Alabama frontiersmen in the Mississippi Territory during the Creek Indian War. In 1818 Alabamians named Blount county in his honor.

51

Jackson threatens to shoot the first man who deserts during the Creek campaign of 1813. This incident is reported to have taken place near Daphne, Alabama, where a tree once marked the spot.

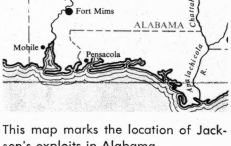

This map marks the location of Jackson's exploits in Alabama.

Old Hickory On The March

ANDREW JACKSON

On this spot, camped his army, October 11, 1813, after marching from Fayetteville, Tenn.,—" 32 miles without halting,"— enroute to the Battle of Horseshoe Bend.

ERECTED BY ACME CLUB, HUNTSVILLE   1951

This marker is near U. S. Highway 231, a few miles north of Huntsville.

David Crockett served as an Indian scout under General Andrew Jackson in Alabama. In his autobiography, *The Adventures of Davy Crockett, Told Mostly by Himself,* he recounted his adventures during the Creek Indian War. In the 1830's artist S. S. Osgood painted this portrait of David Crockett, who was so pleased that he wrote under the portrait, attesting its likeness of himself.

original owned by Franklin J. Meine, *Editor-in-Chief of* THE AMERICAN PEOPLES ENCYCLO

DAVID CROCKETT.

I am happy to acknowledge this to be the only correct likeness that has been taken of me.

David Crockett

Selocta, a Creek chief friendly to the Americans, served as a scout to Jackson in his campaign in Alabama. Around his neck hangs a medal bearing a portrait of President John Quincy Adams.

Smithsonian Institute, Bureau of Ethnology

BATTLE OF HORSESHOE BEND

By March of 1814 the rebelling Creeks were desperate. In one great final effort to repulse Old Hickory, one thousand Creek warriors assembled at the village of Tohepeka on the Tallapoosa river. The cunning and powerful Chief Menawa took command. Menawa showed military skill by ordering log breastworks erected to protect the single land approach, and he also sent women and children down the river and had canoes hidden along the river if retreat became necessary.

Jackson's forces consisted of two thousand infantry, seven hundred cavalry, and six hundred Cherokee Indians plus a few friendly Creeks under the command of General John Coffee. At 6:30 on the morning of March 27, 1814, Jackson and his men were poised for battle at the mouth of Horseshoe Bend. General Coffee, with the cavalry and the Indians, forded the river and surrounded the peninsula to cut off any retreat over the Tallapoosa. Jackson had placed his two guns on a hill about eighty yards from the Indians' breastworks. The cannon balls had little effect against the log breastworks, and the Red Sticks firing through the portholes of the barricade menaced Jackson's artillerymen.

At 12:30 P.M. Jackson ordered the cannon fire to stop, and the infantry moved against the barricade. The 39th Regiment reached the ramparts first, and Ensign Sam Houston, waving his sword, led his men over the log breastworks. Houston was immediately attacked by a handful of Indians, however, and was fighting them off with his sword when an arrow struck his thigh. Fellow soldiers rescued Houston, but Jackson ordered him not to return to battle.

Fighting by the side of Ensign Houston when the breastworks were stormed was Major Lemuel Montgomery, who fell dead of a musket shot in his head. Gradually the Indian ranks thinned before greater numbers and better equipment, but the beleaguered braves refused to make formal surrender.

By nightfall the Creek resistance was at an end except for one band of desperate warriors entrenched at the bottom of a ravine. When General Jackson called for volunteers to storm them, the wounded Houston led his platoon down the hill before Jackson could stop him. The Indians, shooting from portholes, found Houston an easy target. One ball shattered his right arm; another, his right shoulder. As his men retreated Houston, still under fire, dragged himself back up the ravine. General Jackson then destroyed the Indian stronghold by setting fire to it with burning arrows. Scattered over the field were 557 dead or dying Creeks; another 300 were shot trying to escape across the river. Menawa, though badly wounded, was one of the few survivors. His motionless body was passed over for dead as he lay on the battlefield. Reviving after dark, he made his way to the river's edge and escaped by canoe.

Not only was the battle of Horseshoe Bend one of the most important battles of the War of 1812, but it was also a decisive battle in the history of the United States. On that one day the power of the Southeastern Indian was broken forever.

Alabama Bureau of Publicity and Information

This aerial view clearly shows Horseshoe Bend in the Tallapoosa river.

54

First waves of United States militia storm the Indian breastworks at the battle of Horseshoe Bend. In the foreground Major Lemuel Montgomery is dead, and Ensign Sam Houston, center, has been hit by an arrow in the thigh. From a diorama at Horseshoe Bend National Military Park.

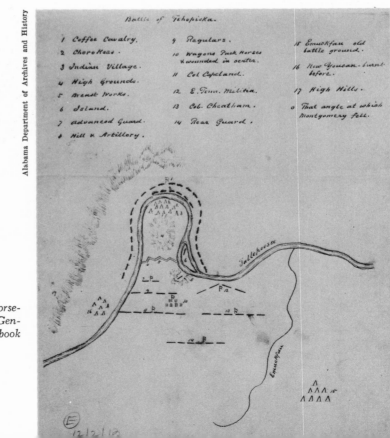

Battle of Tehopiska.

1 Coffee Cavalry.
2 Cherokees.
3 Indian Village.
4 High Grounds.
5 Breast Works.
6 Island.
7 Advanced Guard.
8 Hill & Artillery.

9 Regulars.
10 Wagons Pack Horses & wounded in center.
11 Col. Copeland.
12 E. Tenn. Militia.
13 Col. Cheatham.
14 Rear Guard.

15 Emuckfau old battle ground.
16 New Youcan - burnt before.
17 High Hills.
0 That angle at which Montgomery fell.

Sketch of the Battle of Horseshoe Bend taken from General Coffee's field notebook

55

(Continued)

KNIFE OF WILLIAM WEATHER-FORD. Descendents of William Weatherford presented this typical pioneer knife to the Alabama Department of Archives and History.

Creek chief William Weatherford rode to Fort Toulouse and surrendered to Jackson after the Battle of Horseshoe Bend. The soldiers wanted Weatherford killed on the spot, but Jackson respected his voluntary surrender. Weatherford lived out his life in peace as a farmer in south Alabama.

The Battle of Horseshoe Bend almost cost Sam Houston his life at age twenty-one, but he lived to become twice president of the Republic of Texas and first governor of the state of Texas. In 1840 Houston returned to Alabama to marry Margaret Moffatt Lea, daughter of a Baptist minister in Marion. This photograph shows him at the height of his political career.

OLD TUDOR ROSE CANNON CAPTURED BY ANDREW JACKSON FROM THE BRITISH FLAGSHIP HERMES, DURING THE WAR OF 1812, AFTER THE HERMES WAS SUNK DURING THE BATTLE HERE. THIS OLD CANNON HAS UPON IT THE BRITISH ROYAL CROWN, PLACED ABOVE THE ROSE OF TUDOR, WHICH WAS THE COAT OF ARMS OF HENRY 7-TH AND WAS 90 YEARS OLD WHEN GEORGE WASHINGTON STEPPED INTO THE WHITE HOUSE.

This cannon at Fort Morgan was taken from the British Flagship *Hermes*, sunk near the fort by General Jackson. Jackson arrived at Mobile in 1815 just in time to defeat a British sea and land attack.

Jim Boy

Jim Boy, chief of the Atossees, was born in 1793 on the Tallapoosa river in the Creek nation. He commanded the hostile Creeks, the Red Sticks, at the Battle of Burnt Corn, March 27, 1813. At the end of the Creek War, however, Jim Boy joined with William McIntosh in the campaign against the Seminole Indians in Florida, where he fought for several years. On his return from Florida, Jim Boy found that his family had been moved West in the emigration of the Creeks and that all his property had been confiscated. Four of his nine children had died on the Trail of Tears when a steamboat sank while crossing the Mississippi river. Jim Boy remained in Alabama, making his home near Wetumpka, where he died in 1851.

McKenney and Hall Portraits

When Thomas L. McKenney became head of the Bureau of Indian Affairs in 1824, he began immediately to enlarge the government collection of Indian portraits. He realized the Indians were a vanishing race. McKenney commissioned the well-known artist, Charles Bird King of Washington, to paint the portraits of the Indian chiefs who during the 1820's and 1830's came to Washington in great numbers. King, a former student of Benjamin West, was paid about twenty dollars for each Indian head that he painted. He built color harmonies around the Indians' skin and their picturesque dress and ornaments. King never saw his Indian subjects in their natural habitat.

He realized he had no real understanding of the Indians who posed so willingly but uneasily for their portraits in a foreign city. Nevertheless, King caught the spirit of a people in the process of being civilized.

Commissioner McKenney and publisher James Hall used many of these Indian paintings as models for lithographs in their monumental three-volume work, *The Indian Tribes of North America*, published between 1838-1842. A fire at the Smithsonian Institution in 1865 destroyed the Indian Gallery and with it most of King's portraits. Shown on these pages from the McKenney and Hall book are some of the famous Indian chiefs of the Alabama area.

Yoholomicco

Yoholomicco, born about 1788 in the Creek nation, was the chief of Yufala Town, located on the Tallapoosa river two miles below Okfuskee. He championed the cause of the Americans and served with William McIntosh in the Creek Indian War. Yoholomicco was a delegate from the Creek nation to Washington in 1826, at which time this McKenney and Hall portrait was painted. He educated his children in American schools and brought them up in the American way of life. He died in 1838 on the Trail of Tears.

Mistippee

Mistippee, son of Yoholomicco, was about thirteen years old when he accompanied his father to Washington in 1826. The bow and arrows and the colorful tattooing make an appealing picture of a handsome Indian youth.

Opothleyaholo

Opothleyaholo, born in Tuckabatchee on the Tallapoosa river, rose to the high position of Speaker of the Councils of the Upper Creek towns. He participated in the Treaty of Indian Springs in 1825 and attempted to keep William McIntosh from ceding any part of the Creek country to the United States. He warned McIntosh of the fate that awaited him if he signed the treaty. Opothleyaholo was at the head of the Creek chiefs who went to Washington to protest the validity of the Indian Springs Treaty. He opposed the enforced migration of the Creeks from their native land, but he went west with his people and there continued as a chief speaker of the nation. During the Civil War the Creeks were divided in their loyalty; Opothleyaholo fought with the Federals. He died in 1866 in Kansas.

Paddy Carr

Paddy Carr accompanied Opothleyaholo to Washington as an interpreter in 1826. He sat for this portrait while on that mission. Of unusual interest is the tattooing on his left cheek featuring a heart in a circle.

59

(Continued)

Sequoya

Sequoya, born around 1770 in the Cherokee nation, was the son of a German trader and Cherokee woman. About 1816 Sequoya moved to Willstown, in present DeKalb county near Fort Payne. In 1820 while at Willstown he invented an alphabet representing eighty-six syllables suited to the Cherokee language. His invention of the alphabet made an invaluable contribution to the Cherokees; they were soon teaching it to each other along the roadside and in their cabins. In this portrait Sequoya is holding a tablet showing his alphabet. Around his neck hangs a silver medal presented to him by the Cherokee nation in 1824 in honor of his achievement. The giant Sequoya trees of California are named for him.

John Ross

John Ross, one of the greatest Cherokee chiefs, was born in Alabama at Turkey Town on the Coosa river, opposite Centre. He became an adjutant in the Cherokee regiment of Colonel Giddon Morgan during the Creek Indian War and fought with that regiment in the Battle of Horseshoe Bend.

Tahchee, born in 1790 at Turkey Town on the Coosa river, was a Cherokee chief and served as a guide for United States troops before the Cherokee removal.

Osceola

The most frequently pictured southern Indian was Osceola, Seminole chief. He was born on the Tallapoosa river in the Creek nation about 1800 of a half-breed Scot father and a Creek mother. As the homesteading Americans claimed Creek land, Osceola and his family migrated into Florida, where he led the Seminoles in their fight against the United States. This colorful portrait depicts Osceola in a typical Indian hunting skirt reaching to the knees. A turban of red cloth with three ostrich plumes encircles his head. Hanging from his neck are three silver gorgets which Osceola wore in all of his portraits. Across his shoulders is a bandoleer of dark green cloth with beaded designs in green and red. The same design is repeated in the waistband to which a red sash has been added. The leggings are secured with beaded garters tied in the front.

*This log cabin with its split-rail fence stands on
Monte Sano mountain overlooking Huntsville.*

PIONEER ALABAMA

By the Treaty of Fort Jackson, 1814, the Indians relinquished much of their land, and Alabama opened for homesteading. Among early proponents of the Alabama area were soldiers who fought with Old Hickory and carried home with them wondrous tales of the rich land waiting to be claimed. People poured into Alabama in numbers that rivaled the Western gold rushes of later years. The great Alabama migration of 1817-1818 brought not only homesteaders but also speculators to claim the public land formerly owned by Indians. As soon as surveyors charted the land, the government announced its sale at public auction. Buyers had to pay only a small amount down to purchase land, and they could pay this in bank notes that frequently and literally were worth less than the paper on which they were printed. The speculators formed land companies that bought without seeing it large land acreage. Many a homesteader found that the land he had cleared and now claimed by squatters' rights was being bought from under him by one of these companies. Even if he made the trip to bid at an auction, he could not compete with the bids of the land speculators. In many cases he found it cheaper to pay speculators "hush money" than to bid against them.

Hall, Forty Etchings from Sketches made in North America, 1829

A squatter holding his Kentucky rifle poses with two Indian chiefs whose land he may have claimed.

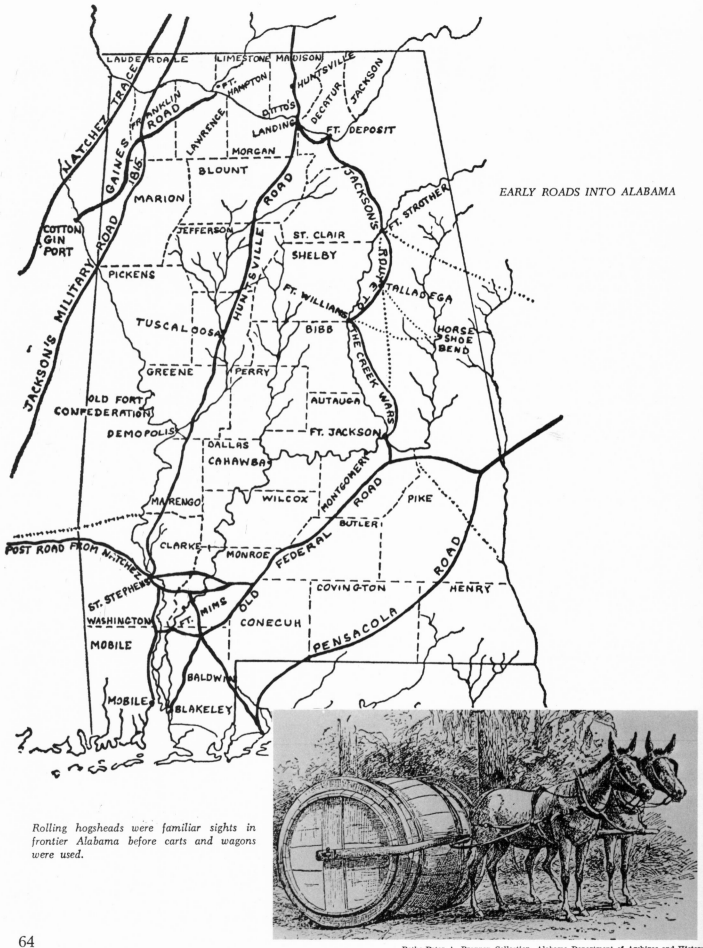

EARLY ROADS INTO ALABAMA

NATCHEZ TRACE
FRANKLIN ROAD
GAINES 1816
JACKSON'S MILITARY ROAD
COTTON GIN PORT
HUNTSVILLE ROAD
JACKSON'S ROUTE TO
THE CREEK WARS
OLD FORT CONFEDERATION
DEMOPOLIS
POST ROAD FROM NATCHEZ
OLD FEDERAL ROAD
MONTGOMERY ROAD
PENSACOLA ROAD

LAUDERDALE
LIMESTONE MADISON
PT. HAMPTON
HUNTSVILLE JACKSON
DITTO'S LANDING DECATUR
FT. DEPOSIT
LAWRENCE
MORGAN
BLOUNT
MARION
FT. STROTHER
JEFFERSON
ST. CLAIR
SHELBY
PICKENS
FT. WILLIAMS
TALLADEGA
TUSCALOOSA
BIBB
HORSE SHOE BEND
GREENE
PERRY
AUTAUGA
FT. JACKSON
MARENGO
DALLAS
CAHAWBA
WILCOX
PIKE
BUTLER
CLARKE
MONROE
COVINGTON
HENRY
ST. STEPHENS
WASHINGTON
FT. MIMS
CONECUH
MOBILE
MOBILE
BALDWIN
BLAKELEY

Rolling hogsheads were familiar sights in frontier Alabama before carts and wagons were used.

64

Both: Peter A. Brannon Collection, Alabama Department of Archives and History

Gosse, Letters From Alabama

By Foot, Horse, and Wagon

Pleasant Hill, pioneer town in south Alabama

Most of these early Alabama pioneers came overland in wagon trains from the older Southern states of Virginia, South Carolina, Georgia, and Tennessee. The earliest wagon trains arrived on roads that were old Indian trails made passable by Jackson's army. For those hardier and braver pioneers who traveled alone over Indian trails packhorses were the answer. But river travel was usually better than either early roads or trails. Utilizing the rivers, settlers sometimes entered the Alabama area on flatboats or improved rafts. In many sections they could make the rafts from large canes that grew along the river banks. If rivers could not be walked through or swum across, settlers built these cane rafts for ferrying to the opposite shore. After 1800 wooden ferries began to operate on the larger Alabama rivers.

As settlements arose farther and farther inland from river banks, the single most important mode of transportation in the new area became Federal Roads. The major Federal Road in the Southeast developed from a system of Indian trails. Pioneer builders of the famous Federal Road in the southeast United States cut a series of three notches along the trail to identify it. Thus pioneers sometimes called this Federal Road the "Three Chopped Way." It ran from the Ocmulgee river in Georgia to Mim's Ferry on the Alabama down to St. Stephens on the Tombigbee. In 1807 the pioneer builders of this road extended it westward from St. Stephens to the Territorial capital at Natchez. The "Three Chopped Way" connected the Eastern states with the settlements in the Alabama-Tombigbee basin and the lower Mississippi. By 1812 Federal troops had expanded the path into a wagon road. However, as late as 1817

South Carolina immigrants had to widen the road in some places in order to get their wagons through the underbrush.

Just above the northwest corner of present Alabama was the "Natchez Trace," over which many settlers from the Northern states moved to Natchez and the Tombigbee settlements. The Natchez Trace, first Federal Road through the Alabama country, extended from Nashville to Natchez, and crossed the Tennessee river at Colbert's Landing, a few miles below Muscle Shoals. From Knoxville and Chattanooga immigrants could come to Nashville and on over the Natchez Trace into west Alabama. A route in this general area less popular than the Natchez Trace was along the Gaines Road from the Tennessee river to the Tombigbee.

After the construction of a Natchez Trace spur down into Madison county, the main body of pioneers came into Alabama directly from the northeast, rather than going farther west and coming down through Nashville. From Chattanooga, northeast of Alabama, pioneers could float down the Tennessee to Gunter's or Ditto's landings or to Fort Deposit. After the Cherokee cession of 1810 there was a road that extended from Fort Deposit along the Jackson Trail and on across Sand Mountain into Georgia. Another important road extending from Ditto's Landing on the Tennessee river south through Alabama was the Huntsville Road. Before the War of 1812 it was an Indian trail leading from Ditto's Landing to Mud Town, an Indian village, on the Cahawba. The Huntsville Road, extending from Huntsville through Jones Valley by present Birmingham to Tuscaloosa, was as indispensable to north Alabama as the Federal Road was farther south.

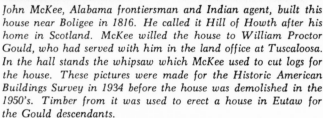

John McKee, Alabama frontiersman and Indian agent, built this house near Boligee in 1816. He called it Hill of Howth after his home in Scotland. McKee willed the house to William Proctor Gould, who had served with him in the land office at Tuscaloosa. In the hall stands the whipsaw which McKee used to cut logs for the house. These pictures were made for the Historic American Buildings Survey in 1934 before the house was demolished in the 1950's. Timber from it was used to erect a house in Eutaw for the Gould descendants.

Safety from Indians, availability of drinking water, a natural opening in the thick overhanging forests, and a picturesque view were often the criteria for selecting an Alabama site on which to build a cabin. Lucky was the pioneer who found a site pleasing on all counts. As soon as a location was chosen, rapid construction of a cabin was not only desirable but a matter of safety. For building a cabin the pioneer selected trees about ten inches thick as ideal for his broadaxe. When perhaps a hundred logs had been felled, neighbors would be asked to a "log raisin." Such "raisins" became a favorite social occasion. Families traveling from a distance of thirty miles or more often camped in the woods or stayed with nearby neighbors as long as four days to a week, the usual length of time required to "raise" a cabin. On the first day the work usually consisted of cutting logs from the felled trees, then "snaking" them to the site with horses or oxen. Ordinarily the finished cabin would be about twenty feet long by sixteen feet wide. Two huge logs, laid parallel the length of the house, would serve as the main foundation. If there was to be a wooden floor, it was made with half-logs, called puncheons, laid flat-side-up with their ends resting on the foundation logs. However, few early cabins had a better floor than the ground itself. Some of the settlers brought with them whipsaws with which they cut the puncheons.

On the second day the neighbors gathered to construct the cabin walls. Four experts acted as corner men. The rest of the men supplied the muscle needed to roll twenty-two-foot logs up inclined poles that became steeper as the wall grew. The corner men used their axes to cut saddle-shaped notches in both sides of each end of each log. The notches locked the logs

in place and at the same time reduced the space between them. This space was made tight with a mixture of clay and lime. Some pioneers left the bark on the poles. The roof was usually made of clapboards that had been rived from logs by hand; as a rule the clapboards overlapped like shingles. Some cabins had bark roofs or brush roofs, both of which leaked more than the clapboard. The earliest cabins usually had no chimneys and no constructed fireplaces. The fire burned on the dirt floor, and the smoke escaped through a hole in the roof as it did from an Indian cabin. However, most cabins that have survived show a fireplace built on one end. Chimneys were made of sticks and clay in the Bigbee settlement; the rocks were not suitable for building chimneys as they were in the central part of the state and the Tennessee valley. Settlers in the Tombigbee area often took large quantities of shells found in caves and pulverized the shells in order to make a good lime for building use.

The finishing of the cabin was usually completed on the third day. Priority went to building an Indian-proof door out of planks and hanging it on large wooden hinges. Wooden shutters covered the window openings. The attic was floored except for an opening with a door. Workmen bored a vertical row of holes into poles and drove pegs into the holes in order to make the support for rungs of a ladder. Two more pegs over the fireplace provided a resting place for the owner's rifle, powder horn, and shot bag. A whipsaw was used to split logs for the puncheon bench and table. When appropriate, the pioneer built a cradle by hollowing out half of a fair-sized log of soft wood, with flat end pieces to keep it from rocking hard enough to spill the baby.

Alabama Bureau of Publicity and Information

Photo by Tom Walrond and James Hagood

The broadaxe was the pioneer's most important tool.

This pioneer room at the Burritt Musuem is filled with original furnishings used by Alabama's first settlers. Note the four-poster bed of cherry wood with ropes used as slats. The coverlet was pieced and quilted in Madison county. Of unusual interest are the grease lamp hanging from the mantel, the Bennington pottery cat and spittoon, and the New England ladder-back rocker.

Here Thanksgiving is being celebrated pioneer style in the log cabin of the Burritt Museum.

Burritt Museum, photo by Victory Haagen

Backwoods Living

Pioneer tools used most often were the broadaxe, grubbing hoe, shovel, spade, and plow. Sometimes the plow was nothing more than a sharply-pointed hickory pole resembling a crowbar which made holes in the ground for depositing seeds. Pioneers called this primitive apparatus the "scooter plow." Even more primitive was "shoe farming." The planter would kick a hole in the ground with his shoe, drop in a few grains of seed, and then scuff dirt into the hole with his shoe.

Fortunate were pioneer settlers who had even the semblance of a grist mill in their area. Such mills often became popular gathering places. Wheat was seldom used for bread in early Alabama because of scarcity of wheat-grinding mills, and little wheat was grown for this reason.

In 1818 settlers in the Tombigbee area were so dependent upon corn for their livelihood that corn sold for four dollars a bushel. Indians taught Alabama pioneers how to cook corn. At first the pioneers were apprehensive about the Indian method of treating corn with lye in order to remove the hard outer shell and thus make hominy. But soon "hog-and-hominy" became a basic food of pioneer families. The simplest way to cook cornmeal was to boil it as mush, and this provided a familiar if not overly popular meal for Alabama settlers. Other foods were cornpone and Johnny-cake, cooked on flat stones, unless the settler had acquired an iron skillet. The original name of Johnny-cake was Journey Cake, so named because it would keep well as a ration for the traveler.

In addition to corn, favorite crops were peas and pumpkins; at the Pensacola market Alabama planters could trade a bushel of peas for a bushel of coffee. The fresh bottom lands along the Tombigbee and Alabama rivers seemed to be especially suited for the growth of pumpkins. Sometimes settlers would cut a huge cypress tree, scoop it out in the shape of a large canoe, load it with as many as several hundred pumpkins, and float it downriver to the Pensacola market. As a result of such spectacular marketing adventures they could exchange the pumpkins for other food or sell them for as high as twenty-five to fifty cents.

Even the earliest settlers had cows. They belled them and then turned them loose to forage in the woods. The cow was brought to the cabin door twice a day for the housewife to milk her. Surprisingly, many people preferred sour milk to sweet. There were usually peaches available on which to put the cream. The settlers raised much fruit. Apples, peaches, pears, figs, and scuppernongs grew well. Colonel Benjamin Hawkins, Indian agent, maintained a public nursery for the Indians. The Government sent Hawkins two bushels of peach stones in 1800 for distribution to Indians to encourage industry and thrift. Evidently the Indians planted peach seeds along a high bluff on the Alabama river; peach trees were found there by the settlers, and they named the town Lower Peach Tree.

To protect his livestock and crops the pioneer had to hurry his fence-building. Chestnut trees made durable fence rails. Beech, poplar, hickory, and cedar made good fencing. The poplar grew so large that at least one pioneer, a Parson Davis, cut two poplar trees at Choctaw Corner and made a quarter mile of worm-railfence ten rails high. Fences were often twelve and thirteen rails high. Logs for rails averaged twelve to fourteen feet in length. Splitting the rails was strenuous labor, but a "good man" could split seventy-five rails a day. Familiar sights were horses or oxen pulling a log chain tied to a bundle of rails. Modern fences have posts and run straight along a boundary, but the frontiersman, with space and wood to waste, preferred worm fences which zigzagged along a strip six or eight feet wide. The ground rails lay at the same angle and sometimes rested on stones to retard rotting. The next tier lay on the ground rails and pointed at a different angle; all ends extended beyond their juncture with other ends.

Indians and then early Alabama settlers were often able to find wild beehives in the nearby woods and use the wild honey for sweetening. From salt springs they could sometimes make their own salt, needed as a preservative. When such springs were available the pioneers boiled the brine in hot pots to evaporate the water.

(Continued)

68

This old millstone once ground corn for pioneer farmers.

Florence Times

A waterwheel near Florence

Courtesy of Mrs. Glenn Hart

MY old GIN is now in operation, & ready to receive COTTON, and my NEW GIN-HOUSE, will be done in a few days. I will gin and pack for all those who may please to furnish me with their custom--and it is of the utmost consequence, to have it ready for market early. I can promise to have it ready in good time to ship. I will also give the highest price for

Cotton,

delivered at my gin--None can be received, but such as is clean and dry-- I will receive Cotton for all debts due me.

DAVID MOORE.
Huntsville, Sept. 28, 1816.   16

Huntsville Gazette, 1816

This moss-covered water mill is still grinding meal as it has done since 1818 when the builder, Jake Rikard, opened his business in Monroe county on Flat creek.

69

With Alabama's first settlers came itinerate preachers or circuit riders. Shown here is the authentic Methodist circuit rider clothing of the eighteenth century. Modeling it for the bicentennial celebration in 1966 of American Methodism is a Methodist minister of Mobile.

The old Scotland Presbyterian church at Tunnel Springs is typical of the meetinghouses built in the Alabama wilderness in the 1820's.

Fiery circuit rider Lorenzo Dow, shown here with his wife Peggy, preached hell-fire and damnation to the Tombigbee pioneers before 1805.

When salt was unavailable, meat or fish was heavily smoked, to preserve it. Fish in the rivers and creeks along which settlers chose their homesteads were principally buffalo and catfish, and frequently weighed from twenty-five to thirty pounds. Using trot lines that had hooks attached to short lines about three feet apart tied on a long line across the river, fishermen often took as much as a hundred pounds of fish in one morning. The Tombigbee settlers soon found a market for surplus fish caught in the Tombigbee river. Men working at the saltworks would pay thirty cents a pound for the buffalo fish and forty cents a pound for catfish.

Fresh meat, of course, was near the pioneer table in abundance. Not far from the cabin were deer, bear, fox, wolf, beaver, panther, and wildcat. Deer of this early period were quite large, often weighing two hundred pounds. Included among the fowl were wild pigeons, turkeys, ducks, geese, quail, doves, and pheasants. Mature wild turkeys dressed out at approximately twenty-five pounds. More plentiful than anything were squirrels and rabbits. Also familiar to pioneer Alabamians were wild as well as tame hogs. Settlers sometimes entered the Alabama area bringing droves of several thousand hogs. Swine were the early planter's most successful domestic animal. They roamed freely through the nearby woods, living on nuts and various roots. Wolves, alligators, and wildcats killed some of them, but the thick fat under the pig's skin made him almost immune to water moccasin, copperhead, or rattlesnake bite. A pig often killed and ate any snake that bit him, as well as many snakes that simply happened to be within range.

Rifles were almost as necessary as food and clothes and shelter for early pioneers. The gun that the pioneer brought with him to Alabama was usually the Kentucky rifle, averaging almost five feet in length. The outside of the barrel was octagonal and was browned with acid. The stock extended the full length of the barrel and was generally made of hard maple, darkened with soot, and then polished. Many pioneers believed that Kentucky rifles had more individuality than any guns ever made; their owners often gave them feminine names.

A long groove in the underside of the stock held the hickory ramrod. A brass plate protected the butt of the stock, and the right side of the wood was hollowed out and covered with a piece of hinged brass. In this "patch box" were stored the bullet patches and a lump of patch grease. To load, the hunter took a small amount of powder from his powder horn and cupped it from his hand into the rifle's muzzle; then he shoved the patch and the bullet down into the muzzle to the bottom of the bore, holding the ramrod with one hand as he did so. He primed the lock with a little additional powder and closed the cover over it, and at last cocked the lock and the gun was ready to fire. The average loading operation required almost a minute. Many caves of north Alabama supplied saltpeter used for gunpowder by the pioneer.

To help them enjoy the bountiful food Alabama pioneers brought with them pewter plates and pewter cups, as well as wooden bowls, spoons, and plates. Gourds made the best drinking cups. In her cabin the pioneer wife cooked in the fireplace. Cooking utensils included wooden pots and later iron pots and iron skillets. The iron skillet with three legs and a long handle called a "spider" became a landmark of the era. There were also long iron forks, ladles, and gridirons for broiling.

Pioneers found or produced such an abundance of products in Alabama, they experienced an almost immediate need for dependable markets. Because of difficulties in penetrating the wilderness, they relied upon water travel when possible. Keelboats, flatboats, and barges loaded with produce became more and more a typical sight on Alabama waterways. The flatboat was usually a flat scow with a simple shelter in the middle. Forward and after decks were open to permit the use of steering sweeps at both ends, and footways on either side of the shanty gave space for the use of "settin' poles" to help in maneuvering the craft. Neighbors cooperated in building these crude flatboats, usually right after the harvest. One of the treacherous spots on the Tennessee river where many boats wrecked was Muscle Shoals, described by at least one early traveler as "dreadful in appearance and resounding at a great distance." Often crews from north Alabama, after disposing of their cargo down in New Orleans, would return north again by walking or riding along the Natchez Trace that paralleled the east bank of the Mississippi.

Professional floatboatmen took cargoes down for pay and worked their way back on keelboats which could travel upstream as well as down. They traveled upstream, however, with little speed. Beams fore and aft and two on each side steered the keelboat. The boat would have at least one mast and a square sail. With a strong upriver wind and the sail set, life could become easier for the crew, but too often such wind was missing. More often the crewmen improvised in various ways to move the keelboat upstream, including hard tugs at bushes along the banks and shoving poles with spikes into trees or into river banks. Such keelboat-to-shore maneuvering was called "hook and jam." A keelboat could average no more than fifteen miles a day "bushwhacking" this way.

Larger and more elaborate than scows and keelboats were the barges. Some barges were a hundred feet long and twenty to thirty feet wide. Usually a keelboat needed as few as ten men but some barges needed fifty men or more. On most barges ahead of the main cargo shack was also a forecastle for the crew, and on the afterdeck there was also a cabin for the skipper.

Poling a flatboat up the Fearn canal from Huntsville

Stage Lines and Post Roads

Almost as soon as the first settlers arrived in Alabama, stagecoaches appeared and traveled from place to place carrying mail and passengers. By 1819 there were twelve roads, called post roads, designated as mail routes in Alabama. One of the main post roads led from Nashville to Montgomery, and it was over this route that young James Powell, founder of Birmingham many years later, rode the pony express. The first stagecoach line in the state was operated by James Johnson between Montgomery and Milledgeville, Georgia, where many Alabamians had business to conduct in the land office. By 1840 there were three stage lines operating between Montgomery and Columbus, Georgia, the main connecting link with the East.

The Talladega Plank Road Stage Line connected Montgomery with the Tennessee valley. The Jemison and Ficklen Company operated stagecoaches from Tuscaloosa westward to Columbus and various other points in Mississippi. The same company ran stagecoaches twice a week from Tuscaloosa through Selma to Montgomery.

(left, vertical) Alabama Department of Archives and History

Alabama and Georgia

STAGES,

WILL leave Montgomery every Monday, Wednesday, and Friday morning, at 4 o'clock, and arrive at Milledgeville early on the morning of the following Thursdays, Saturdays, and Mondays.

Good Horses and suitable Carriages have at great expense been provided — The excellent condition of the roads, and the convenient stands established throughout, render this as pleasant and is expeditious a route as any in the Southern States.

The attention of Travellers is respectfully solicited by

The Proprietors.

** The *Mobile Commercial Register* and the *Louisiana Advertiser* will insert the above four times, and forward their bills to this office for payment.

June 1, 1827.

This advertisement in a Montgomery paper for 1827 shows how long it took a traveler to go from Montgomery to Milledgeville, Georgia. If on Monday, for example, he took the four o'clock morning stage from Montgomery, he arrived in Milledgeville early Thursday morning—four days later.

(right, vertical) Owen, The Story of Alabama

Robert Jemison of Tuscaloosa was Alabama's largest mail-carrying contractor before the Civil War.

(bottom left, vertical) Courtesy of Mrs. Ruby Tartt

72

Once horses and carriages rumbled through this old covered bridge at Livingston.

At the Irwinton Inn in present Eufaula travelers between Montgomery and Milledgeville stopped to refresh themselves.

Mail Route from Mobile to New Orleans.

THERE is a line of Post Coaches that will leave Mobile three times a week regularly on Monday, Wednesday and Friday, at 10 o'clock, A. M. for Pascegoula, to convey the Mail and Passengers, where they will take the Steamboat, and proceed on to New-Orleans; returning, leave the Pickets on the above days at 8 o'clock, A. M. and arrive in Mobile on Tuesdays, Thursdays and Saturdays, at 2 o'clock, P. M.—Fare $12.   All baggage at its owners risk.

VANCE JOHNSON, *Agent.*
Persons wishing information will please call at Quarles' or White's Hotels.

N. B. The Boats will not come round unless there are more passengers than can come through in the Stages.   April 20—120tf

Mobile Commercial Register, January 24, 1831

Hall, Forty Etchings from Sketches made in North America, 1829

Captain Basil Hall of the Royal Navy, touring the old Southwestern frontier in the 1820's, sketched this stagecoach. Travelers complained that the coaches rolled and pitched over roads that were either too muddy or too dry and always too rough. Five or six horses pulled the coach, which was large enough for about nine passengers. Baggage was stored in the rear, and there was a place for valuables under the driver's seat.

Courtesy of Oscar Lewis

As early as 1811 the Lambert Home at Florence served as a stage stop. It was then known as Pope's Tavern. Andrew Jackson stopped here in 1814 en route to New Orleans.

73

Gosse, Letters from Alabama, 1859

Passengers watch as cotton is being loaded at night aboard a steamboat on the Alabama river.

Packet Steamers Plied the Rivers

The steamboat foreshadowed the end of the importance of flatboats along Alabama waterways. The building of the *Alabama* at St. Stephens in 1818 marked the beginning of steamboat travel in the state. No longer would it take three months to travel from Mobile to Montgomery as it had when flatboats poled upstream through shallow water.

Approximately five hundred steamboats plied Alabama's waterways from 1812 to the beginning of the Civil War. The Alabama river had two hundred landings and the Tombigbee had three hundred for the taking on of fuel, passengers, and freight. Most of the steamboats operated out of Mobile, either up the Alabama river or the Tombigbee. Some steamboats, however, from the Mississippi and Ohio rivers came into Alabama by the Tennessee river as far as Muscle Shoals.

There was great excitement when a steamboat arrived, her boilers belching smoke and her calliope playing gay music. Captain Cox of the *St. Nicholas* introduced the calliope on the Alabama river, and it became almost at once the trademark of the steamboating era. The repertoire of the *St. Nicholas* calliope consisted of "Life on the Ocean Wave," "Rory O. Moore," "Carry Me Back to Old Virginia," and "Fisher Hornpipe." The

first time the *St. Nicholas,* her calliope in full blast, docked at Wetumpka it almost caused a panic. The editor of the *Wetumpka Spectator,* however, stayed aloof from such vulgarity and suggested that those most greatly impressed were the children and Negroes.

First-class passengers traveled well on the steamboat. For dining they had china, silverware, and crystal, often marked with the name of the boat. An advertisement in the *Alabama Journal* gives this account of the *Henry Clay*: "She is furnished with such neatness and taste, her cabins are very convenient as well as superb and are elegantly furnished. Since her arrival she has been visited by hundreds of ladies and gentlemen who have universally received that polite attention from Captain Hayden for which he is so celebrated."

Not all was pleasure aboard steamboats, however; danger was also present. Boilers were capable of exploding at any time, and such explosions claimed many lives. The sinking of the *Eliza Battle* one winter night in the Tombigbee above Demopolis, with many women and children aboard, was one of the worst steamboat tragedies in Alabama history. Passengers were enjoying a gay party when the fire alarm initiated pandemonium. Forty people died in this accident.

Gosse, Letters from Alabama, 1859

Steamboats made frequent stops at woodyards along the riverbanks where they filled their dangerously hot boiler rooms with enough wood to last until the next yard could be reached.

BOAT LIST.

ARRIVED,

On Saturday last, steam-boat Tensa, Capt ROMER, in 14 days from Mobile and Blakeley, 7 running days; landed at 22 places freighted for Geo. Wilkinson & Co. Falconer, Hall & Goldthwaite, W. & P. D. Sayer, J. W. Johnston, John Bach, and J. D. Bibb.

Alabama Department of Archives and History

Loaded with cotton for Mobile, the MARY steams out into the Alabama river at Montgomery.

Once the heavy wheels of stagecoaches ground to a stop at this old tavern in Mooresville. On the first floor was a commons room, and an outside stairway led to two sleeping rooms above.

Landmark of Pioneer Days

This quaint cottage gives Mooresville its nineteenth century look.

Photo by Victor Haagen

Visitors journey back into nineteenth century Alabama at Mooresville in Limestone county thirty miles from Huntsville. This charming little village has remained largely unchanged through the years.

Pioneers from Tennessee settled around Mooresville as early as 1805 when the area still belonged to the Indians. In 1816 a Revolutionary War soldier, Llewelyn Jones, bought at public land sales the land that is now part of Mooresville. Soon afterwards by way of the old Winchester Road, many settlers migrated into the newly-opened Alabama Territory, and in 1818 Mooresville became an incorporated town. In the 1820's when north Alabama led the state in cotton production, Mooresville boomed. Along its shady lanes appeared many fine homes built by cotton planters and merchants.

Old post office at Mooresville

The McCrary house has an outside kitchen and a log smokehouse.

*In 1819 Alabama entered statehood in this quaint little building
which served as a temporary capitol.*

FIVE CAPITALS

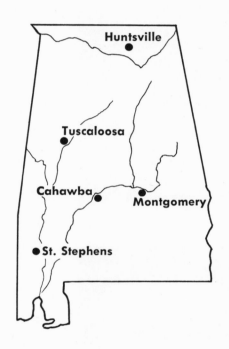

St. Stephens . . . . 1817 - 1819

Huntsville . . . . . July to November, 1819

Cahawba . . . . 1820 - 1825

Tuscaloosa . . . . 1826 - 1846

Montgomery 1847

ALABAMA
TERRITORY
1817-1819

ST. STEPHENS

SPANISH FORT 1789, EVACUATED TO THE UNITED STATES, 1799; DESIGNATED ALABAMA TERRITORIAL CAPITAL, 1817.

HERE WAS LOCATED U.S. COURT AND LAND OFFICES AND FOR SOME YEARS THE SEAT OF JUSTICE OF WASHINGTON COUNTY.

ERECTED BY THE ALABAMA CENTENNIAL COMMISSION AND THE PEOPLE OF WASHINGTON COUNTY, SEPTEMBER 28, 1922.

Today only this boulder at St. Stephens marks the site of Alabama's territorial capital.

Clement Comer Clay of Huntsville represented the powerful Tennessee valley planters of north Alabama who wanted Alabama's first permanent capital located at Tuscaloosa. Tempers flared on this controversial issue in the territorial legislature.

Huntsville Times

In 1817 the United States Congress established the territory of Alabama, a large area of land formerly part of the Mississippi Territory. President James Monroe appointed William Wyatt Bibb as governor and Congress designated St. Stephens as the seat of government for the new territory. The congressional action was in answer to many requests, beginning back in 1803 when the Bigbee settlement had petitioned the government for a capital that would save long trips to the distant capital at Natchez.

The territorial legislature met twice at St. Stephens. From the second meeting came a petition to the United States Congress to make Alabama a state. Such plans for statehood, however, involved controversy. When and if Alabama became a state, what about its capital location? Clement Comer Clay of Huntsville, head of the commission to locate the capital, led one contending force, and Governor Bibb, who lived on a plantation in the southern part of the state, led another. After much study Clay's commission decided on Tuscaloosa as the site, but Governor Bibb persisted in his desire to locate the capital in south Alabama. Single-handed and on his own authority, Bibb selected the site that he desired—Cahawba in Dallas county where the Alabama and Cahawba rivers joined. Governor Bibb, through his influence in Washington, persuaded the United States Government to make a free grant of land for public use as a state capital at Cahawba. Reluctantly, the assembly bowed to Bibb's choice. The last act passed by the legislature provided for a statehouse at Cahawba and a temporary capitol at Huntsville.

William Wyatt Bibb, only governor of the Alabama Territory and first governor of the state of Alabama, did not live to see the fulfillment of his dream that the state capital be located at Cahawba. Bibb, a wealthy Georgia cotton planter, came to Alabama with broad political experience, having served both in the Georgia legislature and the United States Congress. His political philosophy greatly influenced the formative years in Alabama's history. This portrait, painted from a daguerreotype by Dawson in 1897, hangs in the north wing of the capitol.

The Vine and Olive Colony

One of the most colorful events in Alabama history occurred during the territorial period before Alabama became a state in March of 1819. At the close of the Napoleonic Wars many of Napoleon's generals and followers were exiled. These Frenchmen asked the United States to grant them land on which to colonize, and the United States sold them a section in Alabama with the understanding that they would plant grape vineyards and olive orchards. Traveling down from Philadelphia the Vine and Olive Colony, as the group came to be known, arrived at Mobile in June, 1818, where their ship, the *McDonough*, wrecked in a storm outside Mobile harbor. Soldiers from Fort Bowyer rescued the Frenchmen and transported them into Mobile, where Mobilians entertained them lavishly. Then this Vine and Olive Colony of about three hundred Frenchmen slowly made its way up the Mobile river to property on the Tombigbee river. They put ashore at White Bluff in 1818 and founded the town of Demopolis, called Aigleville by the French.

These cultured people, many of them still dressed in the elaborate costumes of court life, did the best they could with pioneer hardships. According to their agreement they planted grape vines and olive trees in and around their log cabin settlement. Frequently after the day's labors the little village resounded with merriment of French music and dancing.

In December, 1819, the first of a series of disasters struck the Vine and Olive Colony. This first disaster was the discovery that the land which they had so laboriously cleared and cultivated was not part of their grant, and as a result they had to leave their town of Demopolis and start over again deeper in the forests. There was hope that this move might improve their farming, but even here their grapes ripened too soon in the extreme heat of summer and the olive trees died in the winter cold. More and more of the French farmers had to sell their land to neighboring and prospering planters. By 1825 the Vine and Olive Colony admitted failure. Some of the group returned to France while others moved to Mobile and New Orleans. Only a few families remained on their lands in the Demopolis area. Today an occasional French name is the reminder of a valiant French effort a century and a half ago at Demopolis.

(Continued)

These pictures of the Vine and Olive Colony were made from the scenic wallpaper displayed in the French room of the Alabama Department of Archives and History. An unknown French artist painted the wallpaper about 1818 for use in a chateau. The wallpaper scene, entitled "The French at Aigleville or Foundation of the State of Marengo," covers the walls of the French room. Beautifully painted in oil on canvas, the pictures are an impressionistic presentation of the artist's conception of life among the French exiles in the Alabama wilderness. Mr. and Mrs. Thomas W. Martin bought this wallpaper in 1938 from an exhibit of scenic papers at the Philadelphia Museum of Fine Arts and presented it to the Alabama Department of Archives and History.

All: Alabama Department of Archives and History. Photo by Alex Bush

CLEARING GROUND AND BUILDING HOUSES. *Crude huts with thatched roofs were erected as quickly as possible by the French exiles. Note the woman with hairdress and costume typical of court life.*

AKING THE LAND WITH A WOODEN PLOW AND ERS. *General Desnouettes in uniform greets the plowman. he left the artist has painted a large olive tree. In 1821 the y planted 383 olive trees in the Demopolis area, but few of grew as the olive trees were not suited to the climate of h Alabama.*

83

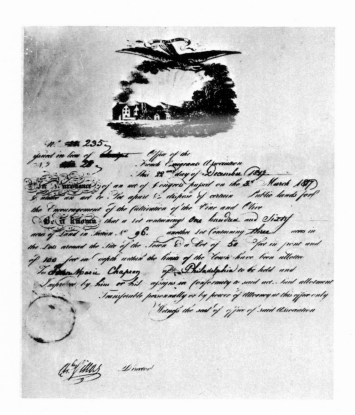

This is a copy of the historic land certificate issued to the French Emigrants Association in December 1817, for the Vine and Olive Colony of Alabama. Among the French immigrants who came to Alabama under this plan were General Desnouettes, General Juan Rico, General Ravesies, and Count Nicholas Raoul.

BUILDING OF THE FORT AT AIGLEVILLE. Shown in the center supervising the work are three of Napoleon's generals: Desnouettes, L'Allemand, and Rigaud. In the painting their bright red and yellow uniforms contrast sharply with the dark blues and greens of the background.

VIEW OF AIGLEVILLE ON THE TOMBIGBEE RIVER
Flying over the busy scene is the tricolored French flag.

Mural by Roderick MacKenzie, State Capitol, Montgomery

The best brains of the Alabama Territory convened at Huntsville to write Alabama's constitution. From this convention came a constitution in which the spirit of pioneer democracy was clearly traceable. This mural portrays Governor Bibb addressing the assembly.

President Monroe arrived at the Green Bottom Inn to pay Huntsville and the new state of Alabama an unexpected visit. Prominent Huntsvillian Clement Clay hurriedly appointed a committee to arrange a testimonial dinner for the distinguished visitor.

Hugh McVay, whose rugged appearance may have frightened some, made himself heard in the constitutional convention as a defender of the poor man's rights. He served as governor in 1836.

86

REPUBLICAN.

[NEW SERIES.]

Huntsville, June 5.

Arrival of the President.

On Tuesday last the President of the United States with Mr. Governeur his private secretary and Lieut Monroe of the Army, very unexpectedly arrived in Huntsville, and put up at the Inn. No intimation of his intention to visit our town had been received by any individual in it; but the citizens solicitous to shew their respect to the Chief Magistrate of the Union, appointed a committee to wait upon his Excellency and invite him to a public dinner on which occasion C. C. Clay Esqr. addressed him nearly in the following words :

SIR,

In behalf of the citizens of Huntsville, we have the honor to wait upon your excellency, and to communicate the joy with which we hail the arrival of the chief magistrate of the nation, in our remote and humble village. Be assured, sir, we duly appreciate the motives which have prompted you to a repetition of the labours, we have already seen you perform in the north, by your visit to the southern portion of the United States. We are sensible of the great advantage of adding practical observation to that extensive information, which we have before seen so happily illustrated.

Permit us to congratulate you on the general tranquility and prosperity which have prevailed, and on the valuable acquisition of territory which has been made, in our vicinity, under your enlightened adminis-

4. *The heroes and sages of the Re lution.*—Many have gone to the bodies of more than mortal freedom the survivors will be sustained their declining years, by a grateful country.

5. *The memories of those who fe the late war*—They preserved Independence their sires had won

6. *Our distinguished Guest.*—rejoice that he lives to dispense blessings which flow from the chievements in which he participated. His country will never forget the man whose life has been so successfully devoted to her service.

After this toast was drank, President rose and returned tha to the company for their kind pressions toward him.

7. *The 8th of January 1815.*—disgraceful to our enemy, as glorious to our country.

8. *Major Gen. Andrew Jackson* He knows his duty to his country and performs it with energy and fidelity.

9. *General John Coffee.*—As l as we remember the 8th Januar we cannot forget the 23d of of De

10. *Our Navy*—Hercules in cradle strangled the serpent.

11. *The Army of the United Sta* A specimen of our resources, w called forth by a necessary defe of our rights.

12. *The militia of the U. States* Freemen, who defend their hom and fire sides, will be invincible when their energies are directed military science and discipline.

13. *The late treaty with Spain* finishes the work begun by the quisition of Louisiana.

14. *Agriculture, Commerce & M nufactures*—The sources of natio and individual prosperity.

Alabama Republican, June 5.

Birth of a State-Huntsville, 1819

On July 5, 1819, the Alabama Constitutional Convention, comprised of forty-four delegates from the Alabama Territory, met at Huntsville to draft a constitution for the proposed new state. John Williams Walker, an influential Huntsvillian, was convention president. Fifteen carefully chosen convention members wrote the constitution. Seven of these men were from south Alabama, seven from north Alabama, and one from the border county of Shelby. The dividing of the convention group between north and south Alabama indicated that again underway was the sectionalism which became the major political issue in Alabama for many years.

Alabamians in September of 1819 held their first election under the new constitution and chose territorial governor William Wyatt Bibb as first state governor. Marmaduke Williams ran Bibb a close second. The Alabama river section supported Bibb, whereas Williams gained his main support from the Tennessee and Tombigbee river factions. In the same election William Rufus King and John Williams Walker won seats as first United States senators from Alabama.

In October the Alabama Convention convened again and remained in session until December 17, three days after the United States Congress officially granted Alabama her statehood. On November 9 William Wyatt Bibb was inaugurated as Alabama's first governor.

The Huntsville session of the Alabama legislature was one of the most important and interesting in Alabama history. Here our forefathers adopted the first rules of legislative procedure. The Alabama Supreme Court met for the first time. Here the first elected governor, William Wyatt Bibb, took the oath of office and delivered his inaugural address.

One of the most exciting events to occur while Huntsville was state capital was General Andrew Jackson's visit. He came down to race his horses and to cement his affection with the people of Alabama. He was welcomed on the floor of the legislature and was given special consideration. General Jackson, already making plans to run for United States president, saw the increasing importance of Alabama in United States affairs.

When Huntsville became the temporary capital in 1819, the fastest growing area in Alabama was the fertile Tennessee river valley, known as the Big Bend. Until 1802 the state of Georgia had claimed part of this area, and the Cherokees and some Chickasaws continued to claim it as their ancestral homeland. The United States, however, purchased Georgia's rights in 1802 and the Indian rights by treaties of 1805-1806.

In 1808 Alabama pioneers in the heart of the Big Bend territory gave their area an official name—Madison county in honor of President Madison. The following year Madison ordered a census of the new county, the removal of squatters, and a public sale of Madison county land. Some of the pioneer settlers were unable to pay the prices of the land on which they lived, and federal troops removed them.

Madison pioneers built a county seat near Hunt's Spring where John Hunt, an earlier settler, had lived. LeRoy Pope selected a site on the bluff above the Big Spring, and here the community built its new county courthouse and public square. Pope named the new town Twickenham, but in 1811 the community changed its name to Huntsville in honor of John Hunt. By 1812 the United States government had moved its land office for the Madison county area from Nashville to Huntsville. After this Huntsville flourished as a thriving community.

Pictured here is the cabin above the Big Spring which John Hunt, a Virginia Revolutionary War soldier, built in 1805. On a small plot of ground cleared from the wilderness, he planted corn and other vegetables.

The first Masonic Lodge in Alabama was Huntsville's Lodge No. 21, chartered in 1811 by the Grand Master of Kentucky. The original building, constructed in 1820, stood until 1918. The present building at the corner of Lincoln and William streets stands on the same historic site.

An early cotton mill in Alabama, the Bell Factory, was built in 1832 north of Huntsville on the Flint river. Part of the foundation and log supports for the dam may still be seen. From its giant bell, tolling the hours of labor, came the name of Bell Factory.

Connally's Tavern, known as the Green Bottom Inn, began operation shortly after the War of 1812 and stood until it burned in 1931. It was located on the present campus of Alabama A. and M. College. In the large valley facing the inn there was a fine race track, where Andrew Jackson, Wade Hampton, and other leaders of the era raced their favorite horses.

LeRoy Pope's
Huntsville

LeRoy Pope, wealthy cotton planter from Georgia, purchased land in Madison county as early as 1809. He helped to found Huntsville and staked his fortune on its future.

This painting depicts Huntsville's Big Spring as looked in antebellum days. Around it a pion settlement was founded, and from it today Huntsv receives its water supply. Above the spring on a c towers the First National Bank. On the same s LeRoy Pope built the Planters and Mechanics Bank 1817, the first bank in Alabama.

This picture of the Madison Rifles in front of the bank was taken shortly after the Civil War.

Through the years the imposing facade of the First National Bank building has been the subject of many pictures. Designed by the architect George Steele and erected in 1835-6, this Greek Revival building is one of the architectural landmarks of the state. The foundation stones came from nearby quarries, but the columns traveled by oxcart from Baltimore to the Tennessee river and then by barge up the canal from Triana to Huntsville. Alabama law once required cashiers to live in the banks where they worked, and for many years the second floor of this building was also a residence.

Slaves impounded by the bank for their master's debts were normally kept in this large basement annex behind the bank.

Crowds gather around the courthouse
square for the dedication of the Confederate
monument in 1905.

Horse and Buggy Days
in Huntsville

A hack stands ready at the McGee Hotel for
the convenience of the guests.

Firemen pose in front of the Clinton street station with their latest equipment, a pump engine drawn by two white horses.

On Dunnavant's corner cash was paid for hides.

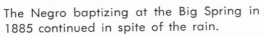

The Negro baptizing at the Big Spring in 1885 continued in spite of the rain.

Cahawba: The Lost Town

Governor William Wyatt Bibb had been suc cessful in selecting Cahawba as a permanen site for Alabama's capital. Because the nort Alabama bloc was still hopeful that the capita would be moved from Cahawba, the territoria legislature appropriated only ten thousand dol lars for a building. Governor Bibb, howeve was prepared. As soon as he received authorit from the territorial legislature to erect a capito he had a survey made of Cahawba, and lot were laid off to be sold at public auction. Bib intended to use proceeds from the sale to hel finance the construction of the capitol. Th auction occurred in May of 1819. Eager buyer purchased lots for a total of $234,856, of whic they paid $30,964 in cash, enough money t erect a capitol with a nice reserve in the bank By the time the legislature convened in Hunts ville in October of 1819 the construction of th building at Cahawba was underway.

On November 6, 1820, the state legislatur met in Cahawba for the first time in the almos completed capitol. Thomas Bibb was acting gov ernor; William Wyatt Bibb had died the pre vious July as a result of injuries received whil riding over his plantation in Autauga county Cahawba had lost its most powerful champior

The disadvantages of Cahawba soon becam evident. In seasons of high water the town flooded easily since it was located where the Ala bama and Cahawba rivers join. While the legis lature was meeting at Cahawba in 1825, rive water swept through the town, and members o the legislature had to be taken in rowboats t their desks. After part of the capitol crumbled from the effects of the flood, the legislator needed no further prompting to decide to mov the capital from Cahawba.

Governor Thomas Bibb
Alabama's first two governors were brothers.
After Governor William Wyatt Bibb died in
office, he was succeeded by his younger
brother, Thomas Bibb, who automatically
came into the governorship as president of
the state senate. This portrait hangs in the
Alabama Department of Archives and History.

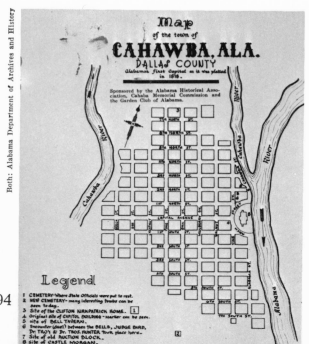

This map of Cahawba, made before the historic auction
of lots in May 1819, shows a well-designed city modeled
after Philadelphia.

The State House at Cahawba

This photograph depicts the stately old Crocheron house, now demolished. During the Civil War General Forrest met General Wilson here after the Battle of Selma and arranged for exchange of prisoners.

The only sound to be heard in once busy Cahawba is water overflowing from artesian wells at old homesites.

There is no known picture or painting of Alabama's first capitol. Hugh Martin, Birmingham architect, made this drawing from specifications that appeared in Governor Bibb's advertisement for bids published at St. Stephens, April 5, 1819.

Many dignitaries worshipped in the Cahawba Methodist Church shown here as it appeared in 1934. Today a pile of bricks marks the spot.

95

Lafayette Tours the New State

When the United States in 1824 invited General Marquis de Lafayette to make a tour of this nation, Alabama's governor, Israel Pickens, persuaded Lafayette to travel overland to New Orleans through Alabama, thus honoring the six-year-old state. The Alabama legislature, meeting in Cahawba, appropriated seventeen thousand dollars to make the tour a success.

In April 1825 Lafayette with his son and a secretary greeted many people across the state. He entered Alabama at Fort Mitchell on the Chattahoochee river, and two troops of state militia and at least one hundred Indians escorted him along the Federal Road through the Creek nation. At Line creek, the boundary of the Creek nation, the Indians turned back.

Lafayette spent the night en route to Montgomery in a log cabin known as Lucas's Tavern at present Waugh. Montgomerians received him on Goat Hill, where the capitol is today. Congressman Bolling Hall led the procession up Goat Hill as the band played "Hail to the Chief." He presented Lafayette to Governor Pickens, who had come from Cahawba to give official greetings to the French general. A bronze tablet set in a boulder and bearing a bas-relief of Lafayette now commemorates the occasion.

That night a grand ball with Lafayette as guest of honor was given in the second story of Freeny's Tavern, Montgomery's finest building. Invitations to this ball were at a premium. Only those of recognized position and influence in the state's official family and ranking officers of the militia were present with their ladies. A New Orleans band charmed assembled guests with both martial and ballroom music. It was a glamorous occasion, flavored with excitement, as Montgomery's elite paid homage to Lafayette. The only recorded complaint was that some taller men found the ceiling a little low for dancing.

Shortly after midnight Lafayette boarded the steamer *The Anderson* and continued downstream, stopping briefly at Selma and Claiborne. At Cahawba, the capital of the state, elaborate plans had been made; but Lafayette, already overdue in Mobile, had time only to attend a dinner and express his thanks for all the honors given him.

When Lafayette reached Mobile, he was again entertained lavishly. His triumphal tour of Alabama ended when Mobile citizens escorted the famed general as far as Mobile point, where a Louisiana escort awaited to take Lafayette to New Orleans.

Lafayette was entertained in this building when he visited Montgomery in 1825. It was then known as Freeny's Tavern but later became the Lafayette House. When the expanding city of Montgomery demolished this building in 1899, Alabama historians erected a marker on the spot at the corner of Commerce and Tallapoosa streets.

Stanley Paulger Studios

96

Library of Congress

Lafayette

This house at Waugh, known as Lucas's Tavern, was once a stage stop on the Columbus to Montgomery post road. Lafayette spent the night of April 3, 1825, here in a bed imported for the occasion.

Alabama Department of Archives and History

STATE CAPITOL AT TUSCALOOSA. This building became the Alabama Central Female College after the capital moved to Montgomery.

Tuscaloosa on the Black Warrior

While Cahawba fought to retain the state government despite its location, several Alabama towns—Selma, Montgomery, Greensboro, and Tuscaloosa—campaigned to become the state's new capital. The spokesmen for the Tennessee, Warrior, and Tombigbee river valleys, emphasizing that Cahawba was unhealthy, combined their efforts to move the capital to Tuscaloosa. They maintained that Tuscaloosa was strategically located in a fertile farming section on the Black Warrior river, a waterway much more navigable than the Cahawba river. Tuscaloosa was also on the much-traveled Huntsville road that ran from south Alabama to Huntsville.

After securing the capital in 1826, Tuscaloosa promptly began to boom with new business and new magnificent homes, with regular steamboat schedules between Tuscaloosa and Mobile, and with a second newspaper, the *Alabama Sentinel*

to compete with the *American Mirror,* already in operation several years. Tuscaloosa sought to become the educational center of Alabama, and in 1831 its citizens helped establish the University of Alabama and the Tuscaloosa Female Academy.

The people of Tuscaloosa were interested in beautifying their city, and under the leadership of Thomas Maxwell, an Englishman who had come to Tuscaloosa in 1826, residents planted rows of water oaks along city streets. Tuscaloosa came to be known as the City of Oaks and Druid City.

In 1846 when the state capital left Tuscaloosa and went to Montgomery, many of the business and professional men moved almost overnight from the former capital. Tuscaloosa remained, however, a center for cotton trading and shipping, and the home of the state university.

This is the Bank of the State of Alabama erected in 1828 in Tuscaloosa. Banking rooms were on the ground floor, and living quarters for the cashier and family were upstairs. In later years this house became the Fitts residence.

One of Tuscaloosa's outstanding historical landmarks of capital days is the old French tavern or Washington House. Built the year that Tuscaloosa became the state capital, it is said to be the site of the legislature's first session. Governor John Gayle lived here much of the time while governor. Because politicians gathered here after supper, Gayle called the chinaberry tree at his door "The Exchange Coffee House."

This picture, taken October 1966, shows the old tavern lifted from its foundation, boarded up, and awaiting removal to the capitol site, where it will be restored.

The Way West Led Through Tuscaloosa

When Andrew Jackson became president of the United States in 1828, the Creeks, Choctaws, Chickasaws, and Cherokees still held about one-fourth of the land in Alabama. President Jackson favored emigration of the Indians to land set aside for them west of the Mississippi river. In 1829 Alabamians elected as governor a strong supporter of Jackson, Gabriel Moore, who was instrumental in negotiating the treaty by which the Choctaws gave up their lands in Alabama. By 1839, through persuasions and threats, white men had made treaties of removal with all four Indian tribes in Alabama.

The Choctaws and Chickasaws accepted as inevitable the fact that they would be forced off their land, and they began the trek westward. The Creeks and the Cherokees, however, were not so easily persuaded. Many Cherokees were now civilized farmers, owning hundreds of slaves and raising wheat, cotton, and fruits. These Indians at first refused to leave; however, by 1835 the Cherokees agreed to the Treaty of New Echota and ceded to the Federal government their lands in Alabama.

The largest tribe in numbers and strength were the Creeks. They owned the most land, and they made no preparation to carry out the removal treaty. It was agreed that whites were to stay off the Indian lands until they could be surveyed and until the Indians who wished to remain could choose their tracts. However, there were already settlers on the Indian lands, and the Indians protested to the Federal government. The government gave orders to the commander at Fort Mitchell to use his troops to drive off the whites. In the meantime, Alabama had included the Creek country in her territory and had carved out of it eight new counties.

Feelings ran high as whites resented being forced off Indian land and Indians resented being forced off their own land. John Gayle, who succeeded Moore as governor in 1831, had long arguments with President Jackson over Indian removal from Alabama. He denounced the action of the United States in sending Federal troops to remove the Indians from their tribal territory. Gayle threatened to use the state militia to uphold the authority of Alabama and the ancient right of the Indians.

Finally the Federal government sent Francis Scott Key to confer with Governor Gayle in Tuscaloosa. Although Gayle and Key reached an agreement, President Jackson lost many friends in Alabama by his opposition to Gayle's stand for states' rights. Many Alabamians thought that the president had no right to come to Alabama with Federal troops to remove the Creeks. These people who resented Jackson's action later formed the Whig party.

Regardless of rising Whig sentiment, President Jackson carried through threats to send in Federal troops to force the Creeks to leave their land. General Winfield Scott and seven thousand soldiers arrived to escort the Indians to the Mississippi river. Some Indians traveled by boat while others went by foot. Four thousand died along the way. Some of the wealthier Indians were allowed to remain, but most of them were sent west at different times and by different routes. There are many accounts of Alabamians who remember seeing the Indians sorrowfully pass their homes on their long walk.

One of the great moments in Alabama oratory occurred when Chief Eufaula made a farewell address to the state legislature as he passed through Tuscaloosa on his way west. Rising with great dignity, he stood upon the rostrum and with no malice toward the white man spoke these words: "I come, brothers, to see the great house of Alabama and to say farewell to the wise men who make the laws. I leave the graves of my fathers . . . the Indians' fires are going out, and new fires are lighting there for us."

As a result of Indian removal, Alabama created the new counties of Randolph, Talladega, Chambers, Tallapoosa, Russell, Macon, Coosa, Barbour, and Sumter. New towns included Livingston, established in 1833, and Gainesville, an important river port on the Tombigbee.

Gabriel Moore

Governor Moore, who wanted Indian land as part of Alabama, persuaded the Choctaws in 1830 to sign the Treaty of Dancing Rabbit Creek, which ceded to the United States all their lands east of the Mississippi.

100

Photo by Calvin Hanna

In Tuscaloosa Francis Scott Key stayed at this house, now the Faculty Club of the University of Alabama, when it served as the governor's mansion. He was the guest of Governor John Gayle in 1833. Key, sent from Washington as the representative of the United States, helped Governor Gayle and the federal government settle their bitter controversy over Indian removal. The house, built in 1829 by the merchant and steamboat owner James H. Dearing, originally had a captain's walk on the roof.

Smithsonian Institution, Museum of Natural History

Mosholatubbee, principal chief of the Choctaws, signed the Treaty of Dancing Rabbit Creek near Gainesville. George Catlin painted this portrait after Mosholatubbee had emigrated to Oklahoma.

Author's Collection

This old map shows the areas within present Alabama where the Indians still lived in 1827.

101

Tuscaloosa-City of Learning

The original campus of the University of Alabama, modeled after Jefferson's plan for the University of Virginia, centered around the Roman rotunda pictured here. The only university buildings to survive burning by Federal troops in 1865 were the Gorgas house, the president's mansion, and Jason's shrine.

Dr. Basil Manly, scholarly Baptist minister, served as second president of the university from 1837 to 1855. Under his progressive leadership the school acquired an excellent faculty and achieved national scholastic recognition.

When the University of Alabama opened in 1831 as an all male school, Tuscaloosa Female College was founded at the same time to answer the need of higher education for women.

Dr. Peter Bryce

Dorothea Dix, national reform leader, addressed the state legislature in 1851 concerning care for the mentally ill. She was responsible for Dr. Peter Bryce coming to Tuscaloosa in 1861 as the first superintendent of Alabama's hospital for the treatment of the insane. Dr. Bryce's use of non-restraint treatment for the mentally ill made the hospital a model institution known throughout the United States.

BLACK WARRIOR RIVER

ALABAMA STATE UNIVERSITY

NORTH SIDE OF BROAD STREET

PERSPECTIVE MAP OF
TUSKALOOSA, ALA.
COUNTY SEAT OF TUSKALOOSA, CO.
1887

ALABAMA STATE HOSPITAL FOR THE INSANE.

Harper's Weekly

As a steamboat approaches Montgomery at the north bend of the Alabama river the capitol looks very near the water's edge. A. R. Waud drew this sketch for the October 29, 1870, issue of HARPER'S WEEKLY before the capitol wings had been added.

Montgomery Becomes the Capital

By the mid-1830's the state capital, located at Tuscaloosa in west-central Alabama, was no longer in the state's most thriving area. There had been a marked shift of wealth and population to the central and eastern portion of the state. This had come about as the result of Indian removal, cotton production in the fertile Black Belt area, and plans to develop transportation on the eastern side of the state.

Such developments created dissension across a young state not yet fully satisfied about the permanency of its capital location. As early as 1838 an article appeared in the *Jackson Republican* declaring that if Alabama's capital had any relation to wealth, population, or territory, its location at Tuscaloosa was "a perfect burlesque." Statements like these incensed leading Tuscaloosans, such as Samuel W. Inge, who instigated a desperate fight to keep the prize.

By 1846 state legislators from the central and eastern part of Alabama came to Tuscaloosa resolved to move the capital eastward. Although eight Alabama towns bid for the capital, the real

contest settled to a struggle between Tuscaloosa in the west and Wetumpka and Montgomery in the east. Wetumpka and Montgomery both had a population of three thousand, both were surrounded by rich agricultural regions, and both were located on the great river system that drained the richest and most promising part of the state at the time. Wetumpka was already the seat of the state's penitentiary and was at the head of navigation on the Alabama river.

In the heated balloting, supporters of Tuscaloosa held their own for some time. Wetumpka, however, finally yielded to the superior claims of Montgomery, throwing its votes to the latter, and on the sixteenth ballot Montgomery won. It was said that Montgomery won because some leading Montgomery citizens came to Tuscaloosa and distributed among the legislators a menu of delicious food from Montgomery's new Exchange Hotel, thus swaying the vote. The city council of Montgomery met promptly and deeded its Goat Hill site to the state of Alabama for a capitol.

(Continued)

This photograph made in 1890 shows the first trolley tracks to be laid up Dexter avenue to the capitol.

The state legislature, meeting in 1892, posed for this picture.

On December 14, 1849, smoke billows from the burning capitol only two years old. Construction was begun immediately on a new building which differed from the original one in having a dome and columns.

The main facade is graced by a Greek portico with six Corinthian columns of unusual delicacy and beauty.

The capitol of Alabama standing on the hill facing Dexter avenue in Montgomery is considered one of the finest Greek Revival buildings in the United States. It is an appropriate monument to those farsighted Montgomerians who almost a century and a half ago set aside a woody knoll called Goat Hill as the future site of the capitol of the future state of Alabama. A brass star on the front portico marks the spot where Jefferson Davis took the oath of office as Confederate president.

PLACED BY
SOPHIE BIBB CHAPTER
DAUGHTERS
OF THE CONFEDERACY
ON THE SPOT WHERE
JEFFERSON DAVIS
STOOD WHEN INAUGURATED
PRESIDENT OF CSA
FEB 18 1861

Looking upward into the ceiling of the capitol dome one can see eight murals depicting Alabama's history. They portray in chronological order some of the outstanding historical events in the state's past. Roderick D. MacKenzie, artist for this outstanding mural, was born in London, England, then moved to Mobile where he lived until his death in January of 1941.

After the Ladies Memorial Association of Montgomery worked to secure funds to build this Confederate monument, Jefferson Davis consented to come to the city and lay the cornerstone on April 27, 1886. The monument is on the north side of the capitol. At its base are four life-size figures of Confederate soldiers representing the Infantry, Cavalry, Artillery, and Navy. On the bronze surface of the monument as it rises seventy feet in the air are scenes from the Civil War days. At the top of the monument is a figure representing patriotism.

107

Montgomery rapidly became one of the most important inland towns of the lower South for the early pioneers. Andrew Dexter and John Scott, who had founded separate adjoining towns before 1819, helped combine the towns of East Alabama and New Philadelphia to make Montgomery in 1819. The soil was rich, the climate mild, and the Alabama river provided a highway to Mobile and the markets of the world. Cotton was king in the Black Belt region, and sometimes cotton bales waiting shipment to Mobile rested in long lines up and down Commerce street. As the state capital for over one hundred years Montgomery holds a unique place among Alabama cities. It has been the scene for exciting and important events from the disastrous burning of the first capitol building, one year after erection, to the inauguration of Jefferson Davis.

John Scott

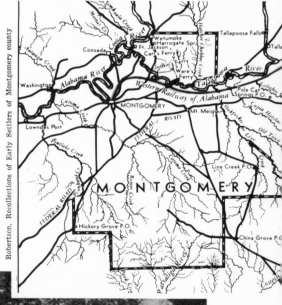

Roads from all directions lead into Montgomery shown on La Tourette's 1836 map.

Pictured here is supposedly the first house in Montgomery. Originally a log cabin it was floated down the Alabama river from Fort Toulouse by the Falconer family. It was set up in 1816 on a forest trail which later became Jefferson avenue. When Montgomery's first sawmill began to operate, the logs were covered with clapboard. In 1899 the house was torn down.

Two Towns Become One

Photo by John Scott

Andrew Dexter

Built at the height of the antebellum period, the Montgomery county courthouse was an impressive landmark before it was demolished in 1958.

Stanley Paulger Studios

(Continued)

Alabama Department of Archives and History

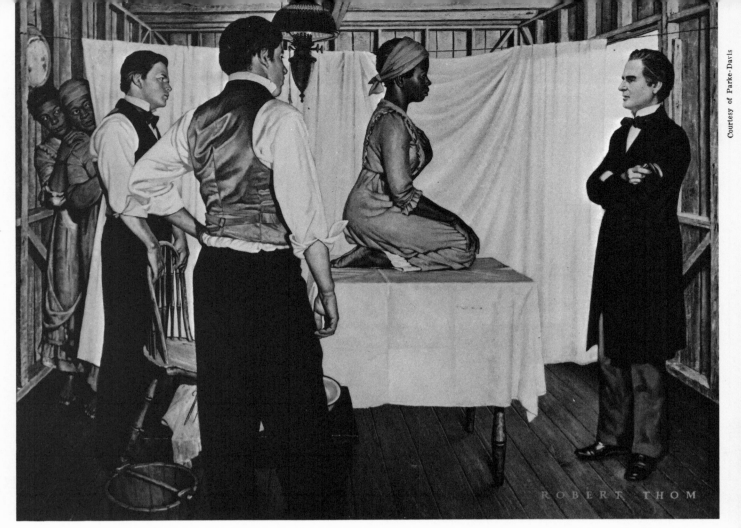

This painting depicts Dr. James Marion Sims preparing to examine the slave girl Lucy in his back-yard hospital at 21 South Perry street in Montgomery. In 1845 Dr. Sims performed here an operation unique in medical history when he successfully removed a vaginal tumor. Later Dr. Sims moved to New York and there established the country's first Woman's Hospital. He became an internationally known gynecologist.

At the turn of the century trolley cars, wagons, and pedestrians make their way around Court Square—the hub of Montgomery. At this spot early settlers watered their cattle; slaves were sold from auctioneers' blocks; and Jefferson Davis began his ride up Dexter avenue to be inaugurated.

An apparently peaceful city is reflected in these photographs made in 1874 as Montgomery recovered from the Civil War and Reconstruction.

Hay market at Court Square

South Perry Street

Reception of President Grover Cleveland at the Exchange Hotel in 1887.

111

The Cotton Kingdom

With cotton as king Alabama enjoyed a golden era of prosperity up to the time of the Civil War. All of the deep South flourished because of cotton, but by 1850 Alabama was the leading cotton producing state in the nation as well as in the South. By 1860 the average yearly income in Alabama for each free family was $8,200, while that of the United States as a whole was $3,670. Cotton built railroads, steamboats, and mansions; it set the social and economic pattern of the state.

Ruling over this cotton kingdom were the plantation owners who lived in a grand manner that has become legendary. The story is told of an Alabama planter who, while touring Europe in his private railroad car, was threatened by a German prince wishing to occupy his car. The old planter refused to move, saying, "Money is power and I've got it." Returning home he resumed his duties as a trustee of the University of Alabama and studied the progress of the two other colleges, the church, and the railroad he had founded and endowed.

Before 1830 the Tennessee valley had been the largest cotton growing area in the state. However, with the discovery of the amazingly fertile Black Belt, south Alabama established itself as the chief cotton producing region. The Black Belt, so-called because of the dark color of the soil, stretched east and west across sixteen counties through central Alabama. It had been avoided by early settlers because the sticky prairie soil made transportation difficult. But with the discovery that this soil produced cotton of unexcelled quality, successful planters from Virginia, the Carolinas, and Tennessee came with their slaves and other properties to this lowland. The Black Belt between 1850 and 1860 became the wealthiest region in the state, with the largest number of cotton plantations and the greatest number of slaves. Important towns in the Black Belt were Montgomery, Lowndesboro, Selma, Demopolis, Eutaw, Greensboro, Marion, Livingston, Gainesville, Tuskegee, and Union Springs.

In this picture made in 1934 Mrs. Amelia Glover Legare, a descendant of the builder of Rosemount, stands on the front veranda. Rosemount remained in the Glover family for over a hundred years.

A BLACK BELT PLANTATION

From his sizable plantation of three thousand acres Williamson Allen Glover grew enough cotton to make him one of the richest planters of the Black Belt. On a star-shaped hill between the Tombigbee and Warrior rivers Glover built his plantation home Rosemount, often called the "Grand Mansion of Alabama." In its twenty rooms he reared his sixteen children in an atmosphere of elegance and splendor. Topping the mansion was a cupola with porches on all four sides so that Glover could survey his cotton fields with his telescope.

A great hall, extending sixty feet across the house, was the scene of elaborate receptions, musicales, and dances. The toddy room was nearby for the convenience of the gentlemen while the ladies retired to the front parlor. Many people were entertained in the formal dining room with twin buffets at either end of the banquet table.

Rosemount remained in the Glover family until 1939. It is now owned by Joseph W. Simpson, who has restored the exterior.

Plantation bells such as this one at Rosemount marked the hours of labor for field hands working on the cotton crop.

19

Gills Thos P, cropper, Pleasant Ridge
*Glover Williamson A, planter, Forkland, 32, 20, 2 e
Glover Allen, planter, Forkland, 8, 19, 2 e
Goodlow F S, carpenter, Clinton
*Gordon S O, planter and proprietor of the Eutaw House, Eutaw
Gordon Wm P H, planter, Eutaw
*Gordon Benj F, teacher, Eutaw
Gordon Jefferson, planter, Mt. Hebron, 22, 22, 1 w--1823
Goree Nathan, planter, Mt Hebron, 5, 21, 1 w
Gosa Grayfield, planter, Clinton, 32, 23, 1 e—1823
Gosa Giles M, planter, Clinton
Gosa John, overseer, Pleasant Ridge, Hopewell
Gosa Ferdinand, planter, Knoxville
Goss John, overseer, Forkland
Goss William S, overseer, Forkland
*Gould Wm P, planter, Boligee, 5, 20, 1 e
Gould J McKee, civil engineer, Boligee
*Gowdey Saml M, planter and merchant, Eutaw
Graham Danl A, planter, Pleasant Ridge
*Graham Charles D, planter, Eutaw, 1, 21, 1 e
Greene Danl M, carpenter, Mt Hebron
Greenwood Joshua, overseer, Knoxville
Griffin Allen H, planter, Mt. Hebron, Gainesville
Griggs James E, livery stable proprietor, Greensboro'
Guard Andrew J, blacksmith, Boligee
Guilar Ed, overseer, Forkland
*Gulley Bryant, planter, Garrett's, merchant, Greensboro'
*Gulley Wm R, auctioneer, Eutaw

H.

Hagins George W, planter, Newbern
Haigood Edwin G, overseer, Eutaw
*Halbrook Jacob sr, planter, New Prospect, 28, 22, 4 e—1819
*Halbrook Jacob jr, planter and carpenter, Forkland, 31, 20, 3 e—1819
Halbrook James, planter, Forkland—1819
Halbrook Burrell, planter, New Prospect
*Hale Stephen F, lawyer, Eutaw
Hale Benj W, planter, Boligee, 11, 20, 1 w
Hales Wm, planter, Pleasant Ridge, Hopewell, 28, 23, 1 w

This page from Snedecor's Greene County Directory of 1856, which lists Glover and his brother, leaves no doubt that planters dominated the life of the Black Belt.

This sketch of the formal garden shows a hedge of Seven Sisters and Lady Bankshire roses. Magnolia trees were placed on the four corners. Planted within the beds were many old-fashioned flowers and shrubs: sweet olive, flowering quince, kiss-me-at-the-gate, honeysuckle, Confederate and cape jasmine, magnolia fuscatti, japonicas, crepe myrtle, and perennials.

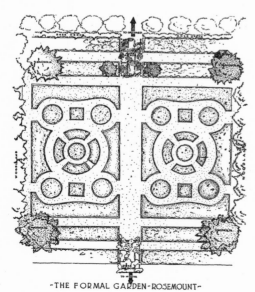

-THE FORMAL GARDEN-ROSEMOUNT-

Smith, White Pillars

This delightfully cluttered room is the ladies' parlor at Rosemount as it looked in 1934 when the Glover descendants still lived there. Gathered here are many family heirlooms. On the black marble mantel is a pair of etched hurricane lamps once used in the dining room.

James Innes Thornton, brother-in-law of Williamson Allen Glover, built at nearby Thornhill this plantation schoolhouse on the front lawn of his home. Tutors were employed to teach the children.

Alabama climate was ideal for cotton which required a long growing season, at least two hundred days free from killing frost. Slaves began picking cotton in August and frequently continued until the early part of January, going over the fields from three to five different times. The best pickers averaged over three hundred pounds a day at the height of the season. In this drawing the overseer supervises field hands at work.

THE KEY TO COTTON

The key to prosperity for the South was cotton, and the key to cotton was slavery. Few Southerners denied the evil of slavery, but in a land where cotton was king cheap labor was profitable.

Slavery came into Alabama with the first settlers. In Mobile city records show that Negro slaves existed during the French and Spanish periods and that the freeing of slaves was practiced there long before the Emancipation Proclamation. After the Creek Indian War many planters moved into the state and brought their slaves with them. By 1820 Alabama had 42,450 slaves, thirty percent of a total population of 127,901. By 1830 the slave population had grown 179%, a much greater growth of slaves than of whites. By 1860, when Alabama was at the height of its cotton prosperity, the white population had increased 171% from 1830, but the slave population had grown by 270%. Seventy-five percent of the slaves were owned by a relatively few planters operating large plantations in the Black Belt. Most Alabama farmers either owned no slaves or had ten slaves or less. The small farms were concentrated in the less fertile counties of the state.

Slave families, helping to separate the lint from the seed, work in the gin house.

Alex Bush

Negro cabins on the edge of cotton fields, such as this one in Macon county, have been familiar sights in Alabama since the days of slavery.

In this old print from a German publication slaves stand on the auction block in Montgomery's Court Square while buyers look them over.

This photograph of ex-slave Hiram Davis was made in 1937 when he was nearly one hundred years old. He still lived at his Peach Tree birthplace on a plantation operated by descendants of the original owners. Davis remembers fleeing the plantation one night to visit on a nearby Wilcox county plantation. Bloodhounds chased him until he was treed. His punishment for being away from home without permission was having to drop down into the midst of a pack of dogs. When he was freed by Lincoln's Emancipation Proclamation, he stowed away on an Alabama riverboat and spent some time wandering. Finally he returned to his former plantation, where once he was a slave, to live out his life working as a free man.

Howard Weeden, famous Huntsville artist and poet, spent her early years before the Civil War on her father's plantation. She had a sympathetic understanding of the Negro, and published several books of poetry illustrated with her paintings about plantation life. Her volumes received national acclaim. These drawings appear in her book BANDANNA BALLADS.

A Runaway in Jail.

COMMITTED to the Jail of Clarke County, Ala., on the 16th of January, 1862, by A. Glenn, a Justice of the Peace, a negro man who says his name is Dave and that he belongs to Mrs. Boddie near Hillsboro, Miss. He is about 35 years old, of dark complexion, weighs about 180 lbs., about 5 feet 10 inches high and limps in one leg from white swelling.

The owner is requested to come forward, pay charges and take him away, or he will be dealt with as the law directs.

R. J. WOODARD.

Jan. 23, '62.   46—to

Administrator's Sale of NEGROES.

PURSUANT to an order of the Probate Court of Sumter County, Alabama, I will sell for cash, before the Post Office door in Gainesville, on MONDAY the 19TH DAY of OCTOBER next, at 12 o'clock, M., two negroes belonging to the estate of Martha Atkins, deceased, to wit: A Woman named LIZZY; and her Child named BECKY.

SIMON M. HOLLOWAY,
Adm'r of Martha Atkins.

Sept. 18, 1863.   ts

James G. Birney, an early mayor of Huntsville, became a nationally known leader of the abolitionist movement in the 1820's. The Alabama press loudly denounced his activities. Birney moved in 1832 to Kentucky, where he could better continue his fight to free the Negroes.

Huntsville Times

This mural, the work of Eleanor Massey Bridges of Birmingham, is in Decatur's Leila Cantwell Seton Hall, formerly a state bank building. It depicts the freeing of the slaves who carried the massive stone columns eight miles from a quarry at Trinity mountain to the site of the bank.

Photo by Alex Bush

Gosse, Letters from Alabama, 1859

COTTON GOES
TO MARKET

From a steep bluff on the Alabama river at Claiborne cotton is being loaded for shipment to Mobile. Before the Civil War Claiborne was the largest inland cotton market in Alabama.

In this scene buyers are examining samples of cotton. Most planters sold their cotton through a factor who performed many services. He weighed, sampled, stored, and sold cotton for the planter. He also served as a planter's banker, advancing him money on which to operate until the next year's crop. Frequently he was a relative or close friend of the man he represented.

B. F. Fitzpatrick,
W. H. Fitzpatrick,

J. H. Fitzpatrick,
J. M. Fitzpatrick.

B. F. FITZPATRICK & CO.,

COTTON FACTORS and
COMMISSION MERCHANTS,

No. 62 N. Commerce St., MOBILE, ALA.

Liberal Cash Advances Made on Consignments

Sala, America Revisited, 1882

As Alabama's only port, Mobile enjoyed an unprecedented prosperity in the golden age of King Cotton. Packet steamers brought
thousands of bales of cotton down the Alabama and Tombigbee
rivers to be shipped to world markets. Offices of factors centered
around the wharf areas, and merchants on Dauphin and Conti
streets filled their shops with fine merchandise designed to tempt
the planters when they left the cotton warehouses. These adver-
tisements appeared in Snedecor's Greene County Directory, 1856.

For the Tennessee valley planter Huntsville was the
first step in getting cotton to market. Transportation
was difficult because Muscle Shoals impeded river
navigation. During high water shallow draught boats
navigated the shoals, and cotton could be shipped to
New Orleans. This picture taken around 1900 shows
part of the block in Huntsville known as "cotton row"
where planters and commission merchants transacted
their business for over one hundred years.

Daniel Pratt

Daniel Pratt, founder of the Continental Gin Company, was the largest manufacturer of cotton gins in the world. He accumulated the first fortune in the state from industrial sources.

Smith, Continental Gin Company

Plantation Cotton Gin and Press

Cotton Industry Booms

As early as 1820 Horatio Jones and Company of Huntsville was operating a cotton mill on the Flint river. This mill produced no cotton cloth; it only spun yarn which was sold locally. In 1832 the Alabama legislature chartered the Bell Factory that operated three thousand spindles and one hundred looms. Slave labor was the main source of employment. Another Alabama cotton factory opened in Scottsville in 1834; by 1835 this factory was producing 4,500 yards of shirt cloth weekly. Much of this shirting went for making clothes for slaves.

Near the mid-century mark before the Civil War, Alabama cotton factories were mushrooming. In 1846 Tallassee had a cotton factory, and the following year Daniel Pratt's mill at Prattville began production of cloth and yarn. By 1850 there were twelve cotton mills in the state, doing an estimated $382,000 annual business.

One of the first cotton gin factories in the country was started in Alabama by a New Englander Daniel Pratt. Pratt, realizing the great possibility of the cotton gin and the need for it, began in 1832 a crude gin shop on the banks of Autauga creek. Six years later Pratt moved a few miles up the creek to build a large gin plant with ideal water power at Prattville. By 1850 Pratt was manufacturing six hundred gins annually. The Daniel Pratt Gin Company became the largest producer of cotton gins in the world. After the Civil War, Pratt with his son-in-law Henry F. DeBardeleben, pioneered in the iron industry in Alabama and helped develop the Birmingham area.

This picture, made in 1875 of a crude Alabama cotton factory, shows the many steps involved in making cotton into cloth.

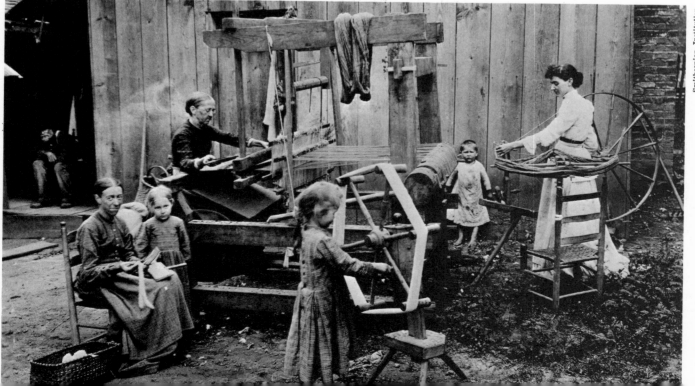

Smithsonian Institution

Shown here is a replica of a historic Southern Railway train called "Best Friend." It is similar to trains ridden by Alabamians in the 1850's. This train set a pioneering record when it left Charleston, South Carolina, on Christmas Day, 1830. It was the first train pulled by a steam locomotive in regular service on the American continent.

Railroads Bid For Cotton Business

Because of Alabama's fine river systems most cotton traveled by water to various ports. In certain areas of the state, however, railroads were needed to connect an inland town with a river or to bypass a difficult waterway. The first railroad in the state was built to enable north Alabama planters to get around Muscle Shoals.

In 1829 David Hubbard, a wealthy Tennessee valley plantation owner, heard that Pennsylvania financiers were experimenting with steam locomotives. Hubbard promptly visited Pennsylvania to investigate, and what he saw made him envision a vast new industry for Alabama—a railroad industry based on steam locomotion. Hubbard persuaded the Alabama legislature to charter the Tuscumbia Railway Company, extending two miles from Tuscumbia to Sheffield. Two years later this railroad expanded eastward from Tuscumbia to Decatur, providing northern Alabama planters with passage around the often impassable Muscle Shoals of the Tennessee river. Tuscumbia-Sheffield and Tuscumbia-Decatur lines then combined to form the Tennessee Valley Railroad, a link in the long Memphis and Charleston line. Horses or mules, hitched single file, pulled the cars along tracks made of wooden rails with iron strips along the top. In 1834 a steamboat brought up the Tennessee the first steam railroad engine for use on the Tuscumbia and Decatur line. On its first trip from Tuscumbia to Decatur large crowds gathered to cheer the steam locomotive as it traveled at five to ten miles an hour. This locomotive proved too weak, and the Tuscumbia-Decatur line reverted to mules for pulling its cars.

An increasing interest in railroad building developed throughout Alabama because the cotton planters were at the mercy of the steamboat companies with their monopoly of freight prices. Many planters complained that steamboat companies "charged all the traffic will bear." During the 1830's entrepeneurs chartered more than twenty-five companies to build railroads in Alabama. Only the panic of 1837 slowed this embryonic burst of railroad enthusiasm in the state.

Charles T. Pollard of Montgomery was the Alabamian most directly responsible for railroad promotion in the state. He settled in Montgomery in 1840 and had the foresight, courage, and money to become a pioneer in Alabama railroad construction. He, together with other Alabama financiers such as Abner McGehee of Montgomery county, made the West Point and Montgomery Railroad a successful business by the time its last link was completed in 1851.

Because of enterprising industrialists Alabama had 743 miles of railroads by 1860. A notable exception to supporters of the railroads was John Anthony Winston, who became governor on a platform that disavowed state aid for railroads. When the legislature passed bills to aid railroads, Winston vetoed them and vetoed so many such bills he became known as "the veto governor." The legislature, however, passed over Winston's vetoes bills to lend money to the Alabama and Tennessee Rivers Railroad and to the Memphis and Charleston Railroad. Not even a governor could halt railroad expansion in Alabama. Only a civil war could and did.

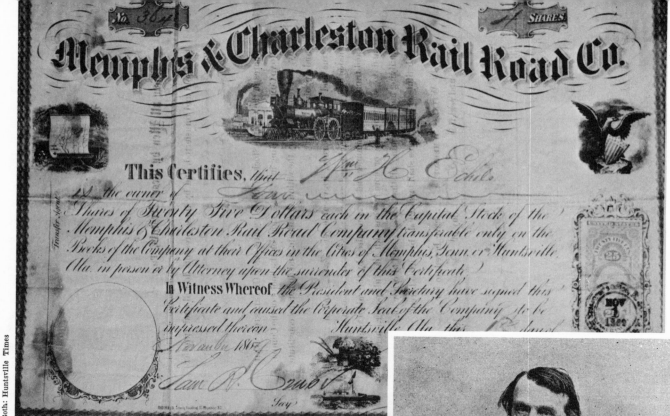

This certificate represents four shares of stock in the Memphis and Charleston Railroad. The Memphis and Charleston, later absorbed by the Southern Railroad, built the first line through Madison county in 1851. Before the Civil War this railroad had completed the laying of track between Huntsville and Charleston.

Charles Teed Pollard

Pollard was the Alabamian most directly responsible for railroad promotion in the state.

John A. Winston

Governor Winston, first Alabama-born governor, vetoed so many bills passed by the legislature to aid railroads that he became known as "the veto governor."

OPENING OF THE MONTGOMERY RAIL ROAD

YOU are invited to accompany the President and Directors of the Montgomery Rail Road in their first trip over the first twelve miles of the Road, on Saturday, 6th of June inst. The train will leave the Depot at 11 o'clock.

CH'S. T. POLLARD, Pres't.

JUNE 3. 1840.

The Bearer will please present this at the Depot.

Reproduction of invitation extended by Charles T. Pollard to citizens to accompany the president and directors of the road on its initial trip.

125

THE ARTS IN ANTEBELLUM ALABAMA

Albert J. Pickett

One of the few books published in antebellum Alabama still read today is Pickett's HISTORY OF ALABAMA, a colorful and lively account of the state from DeSoto's landing to Alabama's statehood.

In the leisure society which cotton affluence created books, music, painting, and the drama played an important role. The United States Census for 1850 showed fifty-six libraries in Alabama; by 1860 this number had increased to 395. The first library in the state was chartered in 1823 for the Huntsville Library Company and was located in the Madison county courthouse. The noted abolitionist, James G. Birney, was responsible for forming the company and getting the charter granted.

Few Alabamians achieved literary fame outside the state during plantation times. A notable exception was Augusta Evans Wilson, who lived most of her life in Mobile and became the favorite Southern novelist of her time. Some of her most famous novels were *Beulah, Vashti,* and the best-selling *St. Elmo.* Many Alabama writers romanticized plantation living, some relying upon humor to make their points. In 1853 Joseph G. Baldwin published his humorous book *Flush Times of Alabama and Mississippi.* In the same light vein Johnson Jones Hooper won recogntion with *Some Adventures of Captain Simon Suggs.* Albert J. Pickett, planter and writer, published in 1851 his two-volumed *History of Alabama.* Pickett, who had fought in the Creek Indian War, was particularly interested in the Indians. He carefully gathered his material from all possible sources. Alexander Beaufort Meek was a well-loved literary figure. Among his writings were *Red Eagle, A Poem of the South,* and *Romantic Passages in Southwestern History.*

Musical gatherings ranged from concerts by European impressarios to parlor musicales and all-day singings. "In the evening by the moonlight, you could hear the darkies singing" and "gwine down by barge to ole Mobile" were songs passed from lip to lip by rich and poor, black and white alike. Mobile lovers of good music organized themselves into the Musical Association and purchased for their use the old Unitarian Church. Jenny Lind, on a tour of the United States with Barnum and Bailey, came to Mobile in 1851. Some Alabama newspapers questioned the high prices being charged to hear the famed singer. Alabama humorist Simon Suggs began journeying to Mobile to hear Jenny, but his money dwindled and, learning of the high fees, he turned back.

Excellent oil paintings were common in Alabama's plantation and town houses. It was considered the "cultural thing" to travel in Europe, because of the relatively impoverished culture in the New World, and in their travels Alabamians purchased paintings, statuary, and other objects of art for their homes. Outstanding art collections of both European and American artists were owned by the Calhouns of Huntsville and the Daniel Pratts of Prattville.

Many artists, attracted by the culture and wealth of the South, lived and worked in Alabama. Transient painters, whose names were often forgotten, specialized in portraits. To expedite their work some of the artists traveled with canvases already painted except for the faces.

Many portraits in the Tennessee valley were the work of an Austrian, William Frye, who painted throughout the state but settled in Huntsville after his marriage in 1848. During the Civil War Frye was commissioned to paint returning heroes as well as husbands and sons departing for battle.

One of the most distinguished teachers of art in the state was a Swiss, Edward Troye, who came to Mobile in 1849 and taught at Spring Hill College. Troye, famous for his horse canvases, spent three years in Huntsville painting the fine horses owned by north Alabama planters. Nicola Marschall, one of Alabama's best known artists, taught art at Judson College in Marion and designed the Confederate flag and uniform. His two paintings of General Nathan Bedford Forrest are among his best portraits.

Many Alabama planters who brought their cotton to Mobile, Huntsville, and Montgomery spent enjoyable evenings at the theatre in these towns. Mobile's reputation as a cultural center in Alabama stemmed in part from its early support of the drama. The Mobile theatre stood on Royal street between St. Francis and St. Michael's streets. Huntsville had supported the drama since the 1820's when the first theatre opened on November 4 with the play "The Tragedy of the Gamester." The Huntsville theatre burned in 1821, but it was replaced two years later. LeRoy Pope donated the land for the new building, and it remained in operation until after the Civil War.

William Frye, antebellum artist of Huntsville, painted in the 1830's this delightful portrait of the three Cabaniss children which hangs in the Cabaniss home in Huntsville.

This portrait of Perry county's Judge James Underwood was done by Nicola Marschall, art instructor at Marion, who spent his vacations painting the town people.

A well-known Huntsville artist J. Henry Strode painted in 1820 this scene of the Martin home on Monte Sano mountain. In the picture Thomas Fuller Martin is shown riding a white horse down the lane to his house. This painting has been in the possession of two of Martin's great-grandsons, Thomas W. Martin of Birmingham and Hudson Strode of Tuscaloosa.

127

Social Life In
Plantation Times

In the Golden Era Alabama's social life became a legend in its own right. Planters often owned fine horses, and horse races were gala events. Dr. Charles Lucas maintained a mile-long racetrack at Mt. Meigs, and owners of racehorses from as far away as Charleston, Augusta, Mobile, and New Orleans came to Mt. Meigs. The Forks of Cypress near Florence won international fame for its thoroughbreds. A well-known racetrack was at Wets' Old Field on the east side of the Alabama river in Lowndes county.

Parties with music, often with dancers in masquerades, were a favorite pastime. Balls were given for the relief of widows, orphans, and immigrants. Such events were highlights of a community's affairs if one can judge from the amount of space allotted in newspapers, diaries, personal interviews, and letters. Dancing academies operated throughout the state. In 1851 Mobile had three dancing classes: one by a Mr. Devoti, another by M. Bauxary, and a third by a Miss Vallee. Mr. Boissieux, a dancing master in Huntsville, advertised that he had just returned from Paris, where he studied dancing techniques. The French had no monopoly of dancing schools. The widely recommended Mr. Powell had several large classes in Mobile with seventy or eighty pupils attending. Charles Chessman was the dancing master in Cahawba; Professor C. H. Cleveland instructed in Tuscumbia; and Mr. Allen V. Robinson taught "the polite form of dancing" in Tuskegee.

Circuses and vaudeville troops attracted large crowds of whites and Negroes. Well-known circuses visiting the state were Spalding and Rogers, Robinson and Elred's, Crescent City Circus, and P. T. Barnum.

Harpers Weekly, November 27, 1858

Horse shows at the state fair in Montgomery in 1858 attracted large crowds.

Alabama Department of Archives and Hisory

Horse racing was a favorite sport of antebellum Alabama. Many plantations had their own racetracks.

One of the most popular circus characters was Tiny Tom Thumb. A favorite traveling vaudeville group, Campbell's Minstrel, played to standing-room-only crowds. Another attraction was the state fair, the first one of which was held in Montgomery in 1855.

The state's elegant "health springs" and resort areas were favorite gathering places. Bladen Springs was a famous resort close to the Tombigbee river in Choctaw county. Guests, eager to visit this area of sulphur water considered unusually healthful, often arrived by steamboat. The hotel featured spacious rooms, including a massive ballroom; there were facilities for two hundred guests at one time. Amusement areas included a roller skating rink, bowling alleys, billiard rooms, croquet grounds, and swings under the trees. Madame Octavia LeVert of Mobile, after her visit to Bladen Springs in 1847, called it a perfect "Balm of Gilead."

Other popular springs were Bailey Springs in Lauderdale county, famed for its Italian orchestra; fashionable Blount Springs between Tuscaloosa and Huntsville; Shelby Springs, the most notable resort in central Alabama; and Clairmont Springs near Talladega.

Point Clear, on the eastern shore of Mobile Bay, was a favorite resort area as early as the 1820's. During the 1840's financiers built the fabulous Grand Hotel. Although the original Grand Hotel burned, it was rebuilt before the Civil War and attracted guests from throughout the nation. By the 1850's the Grand Hotel was operating its own boat between the Point and Mobile. The area was a popular resort even during the early days of the Civil War.

Bladen Springs was known as the "Sarasota of the South."

The SOUTHERN STAR docks at the pier in front of the Grand Hotel.

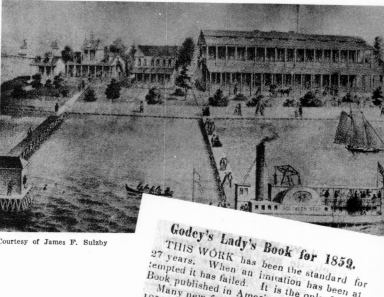

Courtesy of James F. Sulzby

Gramb's band poses for its picture in front of the bandstand at Blount Springs in 1884.

Godey's Lady's Book for 1859.

THIS WORK has been the standard for 27 years. When an imitation has been attempted it has failed. It is the only Lady's Book published in America.

Many new features will be introduced for 1859. 100 pages of reading will be given monthly. Godey's splendid engravings on steel.

London, Paris and Philadelphia Fashions— Godey's one figured colored Fashions.

Embroidery patterns, dress making with diagrams to cut by, model cottages.

Dress patterns,—infants and children's dresses—with descriptions how to make them.

All kinds of crochet and netting work.

The Nurse and Nursery—very excellent articles upon these subjects will often be given.

Godey's invaluable receipts upon every subject. Music, $3 worth is given.

In the various numbers for 1858 will be found the newest designs for window curtains, broderie anglaise, slippers, bonnets, capes, cloaks, &c. &c.

TERMS—Three Dollars in advance.

Address: L. A. GODEY,

323 Chestnut-st., Philadelphia.

Women appeared smartly dressed at these summer resorts. GODEY'S LADY'S BOOK was the standard fashion guide. This notice appeared in the CLARKE COUNTY DEMOCRAT.

CHURCHES
AND SCHOOLS

Cotton not only built railroads and mansions in Alabama during the Golden Era, it also built churches. Revivals and camp meetings of pioneer days continued in popularity, but church members now wanted suitable places of worship for an affluent society. In the 1840's after the separation of the Northern and Southern wings of the Methodist, Baptist, and Presbyterian churches, membership leaped ahead, and church buildings appeared in most communities. In Alabama by 1860 the Baptists had 805 churches; the Methodists, 777; the Presbyterians, 135; the Episcopalians, 34, and the Catholics, whose main stronghold was Mobile, 9. The Episcopal church with its liberal tendencies and aristocratic background appealed to the wealthy high-living planters.

Most of the people flocked to the Methodist, Baptist, and Presbyterian churches, where hot debates raged over creeds, baptism, missions, and morals. As for morals, records of Alabama churches in the antebellum era cite numerous cases of members appearing before church courts and being accused of lying, swearing, cheating, dancing, and adultery.

Alabama did not have an effective public school system until after the Civil War. Private academies and seminaries on the primary and secondary level met the needs of the Cotton Kingdom. At least one good private school, financed by subscriptions and tuition fees, existed in practically every county in Alabama. By 1860 Alabama's prospering economy had built 206 academies. The best known private school in Alabama before the Civil War was the Green Springs Academy, called the "Rugby of Alabama." Henry Tutwiler, former professor at the University of Alabama, founded the school in 1847.

Education on the college level was a primary concern of the church in antebellum Alabama. In 1830 the Catholics founded Spring Hill College at Mobile, and in the same year the Methodists founded LaGrange College in north Alabama. Other Methodist institutions were Athens Female College, founded in 1840; and the Tuscaloosa Female College and Southern University, founded in 1856. The Baptists established Judson College in 1839, Howard College in 1841, and the Alabama Central Female College at Montgomery in 1857.

DISCUSSION ON BAPTISM—By mutual agreement, Rev. W. Mason, Baptist Minister and Agent for the Bible Revision Association of Louisville, Ky., and Rev. D. M. Hudson of the Alabama Conference of the Methodist Episcopal Church South, will discuss the following proposition: Immersion in water is essential to Scriptural Baptism. The debate to be at Suggsville, and to continue two days at least, commencing at 10 o'clock, A. M., on Thursday, 22d of March, 1860.

Both: Courtesy of Robert H. Walston

Presbyterians built this church in Wetumpka in 1835. A balcony in the rear was for Negro slaves, while painted white pews on the main floor were used by planters and their families. The fiery orator William L. Yancey attended services here.

Since 1822 Siloam Baptist Church in Marion has played an important part in the religious work in Alabama. A most significant event in the history of Baptists took place in this church in 1844 when the Baptist State Convention adoped the "Alabama Resolutions," resulting in the separation of Southern and Northern Baptists. The original building stood on this site until 1849 when the present building was erected.

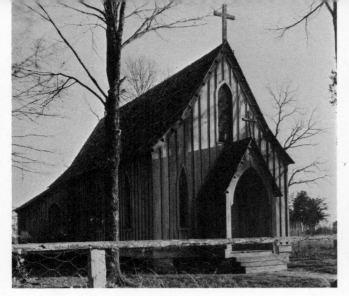

This quaint Gothic Episcopal Church afforded a place of worship for plantation families near Forkland. A potbellied stove stands between the pews in this beautifully vaulted interior.

Pictured in this old print is Wesleyan Hall, still in use on the Florence State College campus. It was built in 1855 when one branch of LaGrange College moved to Florence as Wesleyan University. LaGrange College, founded by the Methodists in 1830, was Alabama's first college, antedating the University of Alabama by more than a year. For several years it had an enrollment twice that of the university.

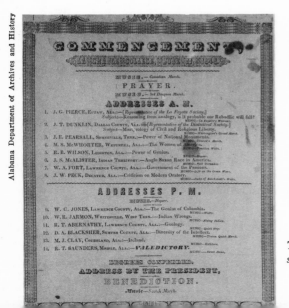

GROVE HILL FEMALE

ACADEMY.

THE undersigned take pleasure in announcing that they have procured the services of Miss Mary L. Boroughs for the Literary, and Miss Maggie Ulmer for the Music Department of the above institution. Being natives of Alabama, and graduates of the best institutions of learning in the State, we confidently recommend them to the public as worthy of liberal patronage. Patrons are assured that every effort will be made on the part of the teachers to instruct those committed to their care, and that proper discipline will be enforced.

The session will commence on Monday the 5th of October and close 1st July next.

TERMS, PER MONTH:

Primary Class,	.	$2½
Intermediate	.	3
Senior	.	4

EXTRA CHARGES PER TERM, 4½ MONTHS.

Music on Piano	.	$25
Use of Instrument	.	5
French	.	20
Oil Painting	:	20
Water Colors	.	15

M. S. EZELL,
H. C. WHITE,
A. J. MEGGINSON,
D. DAFFIN,

Sept. 3, 1863.   26-1o

The 1846 graduates of LaGrange College listened to many speeches and much music in day-long ceremonies.

131

William Rufus King

Elizabeth Cook Hall in 1849 drew this picture of Chestnut Grove, the plantation home of William Rufus King between Selma and Cahawba.

ALABAMA IN NATIONAL AFFAIRS

When Alabama emerged as the leading cotton producing state in the nation, her role in national affairs grew increasingly important. Men learned in law, capable of interpreting Alabama's role nationally, grew in stature with the state. William Rufus King and William L. Yancey debated loud and long in the United States Senate over the question of Southern rights. Lawyers were respected not only for their legal acumen but also for their ability as political leaders, planters, and businessmen. Because of their professional training and experience, they were often prominent in politics; the terms lawyers and politicians have almost been synonymous in Alabama history.

One of Alabama's most famous lawyer-statesmen and also one of its wealthiest planters was William Rufus King. A native of North Carolina, King came to Dallas county in 1818. Alabamians elected him to the Constitutional Convention of 1819, where he helped to write the Alabama constitution. King, one of the first two United States senators from Alabama, served in the United States senate until 1844 when he became minister to France. In 1851 the Democratic party nominated him for vice-president, and King won the election. Suffering from tuberculosis, he went to Havana, Cuba, for his health where he took the oath of office. The only Alabamian to be elected vice-president, he was also the only vice-president ever to take the oath of office while outside the United States. King returned to Dallas county where he died on April 17, 1853, before he could serve as vice-president.

Dixon Hall Lewis

The first states' rights leader in Alabama was Dixon Hall Lewis of Lowndesboro. In 1844 while serving in the United States Senate, Lewis posed for this unusual portrait by William H. Brown. Lewis weighed more than five hundred pounds and his obesity led to the remark that when Congress was in session Alabama had the largest representation of any state. His enormous size necessitated a special chair in the United States Senate. Lewis was the only political leader in Alabama ever to defeat for office Senator William Rufus King.

Clement C. Clay, Jr.

In December 1853 Clement C. Clay, Jr., of Huntsville became United States senator at the age of thirty-seven, the youngest senator of the thirty-third Congress. An ardent secessionist Clay sent Governor Moore his resignation as senator in 1861. In 1864 President Davis dispatched Clay on a special diplomatic mission to Canada where he maneuvered the St. Albans raid. When Clay returned to Richmond after the raid, he read in the newspaper that the president of the United States had offered a reward of $100,000 for the capture of Jefferson Davis and $25,000 for the capture of Clement C. Clay, the latter believed to have incited the assassination of President Lincoln. Clay surrendered to the Federal government, which imprisoned him at Fort Monroe. His wife Virginia persuaded President Johnson and the United States Congress to release her husband from prison.

Mrs. Clement C. Clay, Jr.

Virginia Clay was only twenty-nine when her husband went to Washington as a senator from Alabama. During her second winter there Virginia made a real debut in Washington society. She went to New York for her wardrobe and wrote home to Huntsville that she had twelve new dresses. The piece de resistance of her wardrobe was a hooped ivory lace evening gown, rumored to have cost three hundred dollars. Virginia Clay was not just a social asset to her famous politician husband. She was quite an able politician herself and helped him campaign successfully each time he ran for office.

Mrs. Benjamin Fitzpatrick

When Mrs. Benjamin Fitzpatrick went to Washington in 1853, her husband, a former governor, was the senior senator from south Alabama, and Clement C. Clay, Jr. was serving his first term as senator from north Alabama. The Clays and Fitzpatricks, quite friendly that first year in Washington, lived in the same boarding house. However, in 1860 there was an open break between the two families both politically and socially because the Fitzpatricks opposed secession.

133

Courtview, a magnificent example of Greek Revival architecture stands on the Florence State College campus.

A Certain Splendor

Antebellum houses standing in Alabama today are haunting reminders of the Golden Era when Alabama rode the wave of cotton prosperity to great wealth and national influence. Many of these houses are architectural masterpieces that deserve preservation and restoration.

Architecture can never be separated from geography; and in rich bottom lands made by Alabama's rivers from the Tennessee valley to the Gulf, people settled, planted their crops, and built their houses. In time log cabins were replaced by larger homes and often, by mansions. Prosperous planters—as well as merchants, lawyers, and bankers who also reaped the benefits of King Cotton—wanted houses in keeping with their station. What they built depended upon the degree of their affluence, their background, and their taste.

The architecture of antebellum houses in Alabama represents many different styles: the unpretentious Georgian colonial of the Tennessee valley; the charming raised cottage of Mobile; and the dignified Greek Revival, a style which the Southern antebellum mansion took as its own, giving it an originality of expression not found elsewhere. Two of the most striking additions to the Greek Revival style were cupolas and verandas. Many houses were built with cupolas so that an approaching steamer might be sighted more easily, whereas many plantation homes were topped with cupolas so that the planter might watch his slaves in the cotton fields. The impressive verandas, which have become the hallmark of Southern Greek Revival and are particularly familiar in Alabama, were designed to catch the slightest breeze in a section noted for long hot summers.

By no means, however, do the antebellum homes of Alabama fit an architectural pattern; not only were they planned and built by individuals who left their mark upon them, but they were changed through the years by many different generations with varying tastes and needs. Sometimes a simple two-story log house with wings added became in time a dignified colonnaded mansion. The raised cottage, designed for low water areas, was glorified in many instances with a pillared entrance to please its owner, and a brick colonial was decorated with a colonnaded gallery in imitation of the Greek Revival.

Since Alabama's rivers served as highways in antebellum times, most homes were located either on a plantation close to a river or in a town where a river flowed close by. Steamboats, carrying cotton and passengers, brought building materials and furnishings for antebellum homes. Shipped upstream from Mobile, the shopping mecca for central and south Alabama, were marble mantels, wrought iron grills, damask drapes, pianos, and scenic wallpaper. From Mobile also came trained artisans to execute plaster medallions and mantel designs.

Even though Alabama attracted a few professionally trained architects, notably George Steele, most antebellum houses in the state were designed and built by the men who lived in them. Some knowledge of architecture was a part of gentlemen's education in the old South, and private libraries included architectural manuals over which builders spent long hours planning their houses. With slave labor builders felled timber from nearby forests and made brick in their own kilns. Many slaves were expert craftsmen, skilled in carving and plaster work. Itinerate carpenters, traveling with their families and slaves, were for hire and helped to build houses, staying a year or more in one place, if necessary, to complete a structure. To the builders, who wanted hand-carved mantels and well-proportioned stairways, the quality of the work took precedent over the time required to do it. The many fine antebellum houses standing in Alabama today are tributes to their builders who endowed them with a certain splendor enhanced by the years.

The Tennessee River Valley

Huntsville

After the Creek Indian wars opened up land in Alabama, wealthy cotton planters moved into the fertile Tennessee valley of north Alabama, bringing their slaves and possessions with them. These men, who had enjoyed political and social prestige in their home states of Georgia, the Carolinas, and Virginia, built homes reminiscent of their former way of life. Many chose the traditional Georgian architecture that flourished along the Tidewater while others turned to Greek Revival. Generally the simpler Georgian design was favored, and nowhere in the state are there more homes of this type than in the Tennessee valley. Brick was a favorite building material as contrasted with wood used more commonly throughout the rest of the state.

Huntsville's streets and houses reflect the antebellum period when Huntsville was the center of north Alabama wealth and power. Charming old Georgian cottages and imposing Greek Revival mansions stand side by side. Near the courthouse square in the Twickenham section are fifty-nine antebellum houses still used as private homes; no other city in Alabama has so well preserved its old homes in one concentrated area. George Steele, who as a young man came from Virginia to Huntsville before Alabama was a state, created many of the fine buildings and homes in Huntsville. The Cabaniss, Clay, Steele-Fowler, and LeRoy Pope homes stand today as landmarks to his architectural skill.

Franklin street leads to the old courthouse square.

136

Courtesy of Huntsville Times

Photo by Victor Haagen

Huntsville takes particular pride in the Pope mansion, built in 1815. The portico has a classic grandeur unmatched elsewhere in Alabama. The lavish yet dignified design of the portico reflects the genius of the architect, George Steele. The crowning glory of the front is the pediment with a fan-shaped center design repeated in the front door transom. LeRoy Pope Walker, grandson of LeRoy Pope, sold the house in 1858 to Dr. Charles Hayes Patton. The splendid condition of the house today is a tribute to the five generations of the Patton family who have lived in it.

The Pope Mansion

CEDARHURST

In 1825 Stephen S. Ewing, the builder of Cedarhurst, chose a rolling hill over-looking 132 acres as the site for his plantation home. The Ewings, a Virginia family, operated several large plantations in north Alabama and Mississippi. The dark green of the old cedar trees lining the drive contrasts sharply with the gleam-ing white brick of the house. A drive around the house leads to the family ceme-tery where a few markers still stand, one of sixteen-year-old Sally Carter.

On the recessed entrance doors are the original brass rim locks and doorpull. In the dining room are windows with original panes of handmade glass. The summer kitchen, now used as an apartment, still stands in the rear, and the winter kitchen in the basement now houses the heating plant. The essential character of the old home has been faithfully preserved by the J. D. Thorntons, who purchased Cedarhurst in 1919. It stands today as an authentic bit of **early Huntsville.**

his lovely old stairway has served the occupants of Cedarhurst r almost 150 years.

Many visitors with an imagination for ghosts claim that Sally Carter haunts her room at Cedarhurst. These furnishings are fine examples of a Victorian bed and wardrobe. Note that the head-board of the baby bed matches that of the big bed, which is covered with a hundred-year-old patchwork quilt.

Moore-Cummings-Rhett House

A wealthy bachelor Samuel Moore acquired this antebellum home after the Civil War. In 1893 he gave a reception honoring Lily Flagg, his prize Jersey cow, who had won international fame for her butter-production ability. Lily stood in the ballroom with a flower garland about her neck while guests filed past to music of an Italian orchestra.

Charles Bell, a Negro carpenter, came from Charlottesville, Virginia, to build this exquisite spiral stairway curving around a center post leading to the cupola. Bell, noted throughout the South for his stairways, spent three years constructing the three stairs in this home.

This parlor leaves no doubt that the Cummings home possesses an interior of great beauty and charm. The elaborately carved Belter sofa and chair, covered in apple-green satin, set off the polished marble mantel decorated with carved flowers. Grape clusters and curled leaves make a striking cornice decoration. A bronze chandelier from France hangs from the ceiling.

Both: Photos by Victor Haagen

The Pynchon House

This beautiful red-brick house with a small columned portico typifies the Tidewater influence so predominant in Huntsville architecture. The house has grown from a few rooms in 1835 to a nineteen-room mansion, famous for the prominent widows who have lived here. Boxwood line the walks, and yew trees over one hundred years old shade the house. In the rear a terrace overlooks the garden planned by an English landscape architect.

Many fine period pieces furnish the Pynchon house. In this bedroom the four-poster has a trundle bed pulled out when additional sleeping room was needed. In the corner is a fine example of an eighteenth century Chippendale chest on stand.

The Cabaniss-Roberts House

A tribute to the versatility of George Steele is the Cabaniss home. It is hard to believe that the same man who had created the impressive Pope mansion .also built this charming Georgian structure. Steptimus D. Cabaniss, attorney of Huntsville, purchased the house for his bride from one of George Steele's associates. The young bride had her ups and downs in this many-level house. Dining room and kitchen awaited in the basement while parlors must be kept on the first floor, and the bedrooms could be reached only by another flight upward. As the family grew and more room was needed, a wing with two additional bedrooms, dressing rooms, and a sun porch were added between the basement and second floor to make even another level. An unusually interesting furnishing is the cherry bedroom suite brought from Virginia by Charles Cabaniss, father of Steptimus D. Cabaniss, when he first came to Madison county in 1809.

The Cabaniss home remains in the hands of a fifth-generation heir, Miss Ellen Douglas Roberts, who delights in the care of the house as fondly as the first Mrs. Cabaniss did in 1843.

The same carriage block upon which Virginia Shepherd Cabaniss stepped as a bride in 1843 stands in front of the house.

Both: Photos by Dudley Campbell

The Bassett-Young House

Dr. John Young Bassett, famous for his research in malaria and typhoid fever, purchased this house in the 1830's and lived here until his death in 1851. Sir William Osler, physician to the King of England, based his book *An Alabama Student* upon Dr. Bassett's life and letters. The massive entrance doors with original brasses and a double cross are show pieces of Huntsville. The beaded molding and a brick arch over the fanlight enhance the beauty of the striking entrance.

Running along Williams street in front of the Bibb mansion is this cleverly designed hand-sawn picket fence of cypress wood.

Dr. Thomas Fearn

Dr. Thomas Fearn, prominent in the early development of Madison county, installed the Huntsville public waterworks, the first in the state, and planned the canal from Huntsville to the Tennessee river. This portrait hangs in the Burritt Museum in recognition of Dr. Fearn's discovery of Monte Sano as a health resort.

Fearn-Garth-Richardson House

General Andrew Jackson brought Dr. Thomas Fearn from Virginia in 1814 to be surgeon-general of the military hospital in Huntsville. Dr. Fearn built this imposing two-story brick residence in the 1820's. A classic portico with four columns faces the street. Massive oaks planted by Dr. Fearn shade the house today. An unusual architectural feature is the recessing of the exterior walls producing a paneled effect.

This charming portrait of little Ida Harris Richardson was painted by the itinerant artist, Dufy, probably in the 1830's.

This hitching post still stands in front of the Fearn house. Behind it may be seen the brick walk and iron fence, part of the original landscaping.

144

The muted tones of oriental rugs enhance the beauty of the front parlor. A New Orleans ballroom chair stands in front of the rosewood square grand piano.

The interior of the house preserves the flavor of the nineteenth century. The classic proportions of this hand-carved stair make it one of the finest in Alabama.

Both: Photo by Victor Haagen

Drake-Garth-Jones Farm

In 1828 James Drake built this house in the middle of his three-thousand-acre plantation. Today the house, beautifully restored, serves as the homeplace for the Jones Valley Farm. Many reminders of plantation life surround the house: the old family cemetery, an overseer's house, and numerous outbuildings.

Fifty guests may be seated at this banquet table when it is extended to its full length. The dining room is located in the basement area of the raised cottage house.

Both: Photos by Victor Haagen

BELLE MINA

An old brick walk bordered with boxwood leads to Belle Mina, one of the most historic and beautiful of Alabama's antebellum homes. Thomas Bibb, second governor of Alabama, built Belle Mina in 1826 a few miles from Huntsville. Bibb, the largest land owner in north Alabama and a former Virginian of education and good taste, spared no expense or effort in building a handsome and livable plantation house.

Unlike the later elaborately decorated Greek Revival mansions of the Black Belt, the classic facade of Belle Mina is pleasingly simple in its Doric order, the six columns unadorned and the entableture plain. The columns are so set that the impressive Georgian doorway with its fan-lighted entrance stands out in delicate relief.

Belle Mina remained in the hands of the Bibb family until 1941 when it was purchased by Dr. and Mrs. Berthold Kennedy, who began to restore the house to its former elegance. Since 1966 Belle Mina has been owned by Mr. and Mrs. Thomas A. Bowles, who have continued its restoration. Fine antiques furnish the spacious rooms where once important events in Alabama's early statehood took place.

Bread was baked in the Dutch oven to the left of the fireplace.

147

Inside Belle Mina there are many fascinating architectural details. Two prominent features of the great hall are the graceful curving stair of cherry wood and the rear door with its fanlighted transom. The Georgian settee and the Queen Anne lowboy on one side balance the fine breakfront and side chairs on the other. The Waterford crystal chandelier and antique oriental runner are collector's pieces.

Focal points of the twin parlors are the exquisitely reeded and fluted mantels, considered to be the finest wooden mantels in any antebellum mansion in Alabama. Paneled shutters, oriental rugs, and fine period pieces set off these stately rooms.

The Beaty-Mason House

On a tree-lined street in Athens stands the Mason house, used by Athens College as the president's mansion. Robert Beaty, who purchased land in the Tennessee valley in 1809, planned this house to be a school. The original building was a four-room two-story house with walls twenty inches thick made of brick and limestone. John Mason, who acquired the house in 1845 when he married a daughter of Robert Beaty's, remodeled the house. The front porch was removed and a small veranda with four columns added. A brass knocker on the front door bears the inscription "John R. Mason 1845." The early character of this charming old house has been retained in its restoration.

A closeup view of the hand-made wooden locks in the slave kitchen

The slave quarters at the rear have been made into a guest house. One large chimney in the center served the huge fireplaces in each room.

149

The Warrior-Tombigbee River Country

ARLINGTON

Judge William S. Mudd
Judge Mudd, builder of Arlington, helped to found Birmingham after the Civil War. He lived to see the little village of Elyton absorbed into the thriving industrial city.

Arlington is one of the few antebellum landmarks in Jefferson county. Wilson's raiders made this house their headquarters as they moved toward Tuscaloosa and Montevallo.

Victorian chairs and sofas in the double parlor once graced the plantation house of William Wyatt Bibb, Alabama's first governor.

In 1841 William Swearingen Mudd, a promising young attorney in Elyton, purchased a hundred-acre tract of land from his new father-in-law, Samuel S. Earle. On a knoll overlooking broad cotton land he built this two-story square-colonnaded house today called Arlington. Here William and Florence Earle Mudd reared their family of nine children.

In 1884 Judge Mudd sold his property to Birmingham's industrial giant Henry DeBardeleben, but Mr. DeBardeleben never lived there. Arlington had its reverses until in 1905 Robert Sylvester Munger purchased the house for use first as a summer retreat and later as a permanent residence. A daughter of Mr. Munger, Mrs. A. C. Montgomery, occupied Arlington with her family until 1952 when the city of Birmingham purchased the property and established the Arlington Shrine. Today in the midst of busy Birmingham stands this lovely old mansion with its well-kept grounds and beautifully appointed interior.

Arrangements of wax flowers under glass such as this one in the sitting room at Arlington were popular in antebellum days.

The piano, a rosewood square grand made in 1818, came from the home of Governor Barry Moore of Alabama. The astrol lamps on the piano were made originally to burn whale oil.

(Continued)

Dominating this upstairs bedroom is a tester field bed with canopied top and ruffled skirt. A washstand with pitcher and bowl stands beneath the pine mirror. In front of the full-length windows is a doll's cradle and a miniature ladderback chair and spinning wheel. The hooked rugs, Windsor rocker, and pine desk complete the well-chosen furnishings which mark the appointments used throughout the house.

In the Hassinger bedroom is this French Victorian bed with a secret compartment in one of the pomegranate posts.

Tuscaloosa

Tuscaloosa Chamber of Commerce

The Jemison House

Robert Jemison, who amassed a fortune from stage lines and railroads before the Civil War, hired a Philadelphia architect in the late 1850's to design this Italianate-type house for him. All material for the house came from Jemison's plantation, and the work was done by slaves. Tradition tells of one workman who surpassed all others and received his freedom as a reward. Every detail of the house from door facings to stair rails was elaborately designed. Hugo Friedman gave this house to the county for a public library in the 1940's.

HABS, Library of Congress

Built in 1837, this charming country house, once part of a cotton plantation, stood on the outskirts of Tuscaloosa. It was the home of Samuel Menton Peck, poet laureate of Alabama.

This bust of William Crawford Gorgas, surgeon-general of the United States Army and world authority on sanitary engineering, was made from life by P. Bryant Baker, sculptor of Boston, Massachusetts. It is in the state capitol. On his deathbed in London, Gorgas was knighted by King George V.

The Gorgas House

The Gorgas home, one of the three buildings on the University of Alabama campus which survived the war, is now a state shrine. It is considered one of the best types of raised cottage architecture in the state. Built in 1829 as a home for the university steward, it has served as mess hall, hospital, and post office. Bricks used in the house were brought from England in trading ships as ballast. General Josiah B. Gorgas, Chief of Ordnance for the Confederate States Army and president of the university for a brief period, brought his family here to live in 1878. His wife, Amelia Gayle Gorgas, was greatly loved and respected at the university where she served as librarian from 1883 to 1906.

Courtesy of Robert H. Walston

The President's Mansion

The president's mansion of the University of Alabama is regarded by experts as a notable example of Greek Revival architecture. William Nichols of Philadelphia was the architect. All construction work was done by native craftsmen, even to the carving of the marble Ionic capitals. The elaborate frescoes and medallions on the inside were executed by slaves. One gets little idea of the great size of this house because of its setting and proportions. The cornice of the roof is over forty-one feet from the ground, and the house is nearly sixty feet across. This house was saved from destruction in 1865 by the courage of Mrs. Landon C. Garland, wife of the university president. She ordered the Federal soldiers to put out the fire which they had kindled, and she remained in the house while the university was being burned.

Wide marble steps lead up to the entrance veranda where six white square columns support the portico roof surrounded by a balustrade.

The Battle-Friedman House

The Friedman home, occupying an entire city block on Greensboro avenue, was built in 1835 by Alfred Battle, a prominent Tuscaloosa merchant and planter. Since 1881 the place has been owned by the Friedman family, who have preserved all the dignity and beauty of this antebellum house and grounds. Sandstone blocks on the front of the house have mellowed to a shade of pink and cream; the remainder of the house is built of red brick. A particularly arresting architectural detail is the doorway with its delicate side and fanlights. An elaborately decorated cornice further enhances the beauty of the entrance hall.

The poet Robert Loveman, while studying law at the University of Alabama, lived here with his aunt Linka Friedman. A favorite retreat of the poet was the scuppernong-covered summer house in the side garden where he may have composed these famous lines: "It isn't raining rain to me, it's raining daffodils."

All: Photos by Calvin Hanna

An eighteenth century tall-case clock stands in the spacious entrance hall.

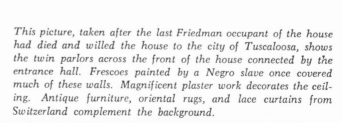

This picture, taken after the last Friedman occupant of the house had died and willed the house to the city of Tuscaloosa, shows the twin parlors across the front of the house connected by the entrance hall. Frescoes painted by a Negro slave once covered much of these walls. Magnificent plaster work decorates the ceiling. Antique furniture, oriental rugs, and lace curtains from Switzerland complement the background.

MAGNOLIA GROVE

In Greensboro is Magnolia Grove, the ancestral home of Rear Admiral Richmond Pearson Hobson. In the twenty-acre grove surrounding the house aged magnolia trees touch the ground. Isaac Croom, a planter from South Carolina, built the house in 1835. Admiral Hobson lived here after his retirement until his death in 1937.

In Hobson's study among his collection of books and curios rests this nameplate from the MERRIMAC.

Young Lieutenant Richmond Pearson Hobson directed the sinking of the MERRIMAC during the Spanish-American War. This feat was considered the most dramatic incident of the war. Hobson received the Congressional Medal of Honor for his heroic action. This portrait by Maltby Sykes hangs in the Department of Archives and History.

The silver service displayed here on an old sideboard was presented to Admiral Hobson during a reception at Magnolia Grove.

The ballroom

Alabama Department of Archives and History

GAINESWOOD

Gaineswood, the Whitfield home in Demopolis, is considered by some to be the most magnificent antebellum mansion in Alabama. General Nathan Bryan Whitfield was his own architect. In addition to the exterior he designed the interior ornamentations and brought expert artisans from Philadelphia to aid him in carrying out his plans. With the help of architectural handbooks in his library, General Whitfield planned the elaborate cornices and columns used in the house. Three types of Greek columns are represented in its architecture. The outside columns follow the simple lines of the Doric. The interior columns are Ionic except in the drawing room where the elaborate Corinthian columns are reflected in ceiling-to-floor mirrors. General Whitfield named Gaineswood in honor of his friend George Strother Gaines, the Choctaw Indian agent. About 1865 the distinguished artist, John Sartain of Philadelphia, made this steel engraving of Gaineswood.

Alabama Department of Archives and History. Photo by Alex Bush

Bluff Hall

As a gift to his daughter in 1832 Allen Glover built Bluff Hall on a steep cliff in Demopolis. Entrance to the grounds was once through this beautifully designed old gate.

Courtesy of Frances Roberts

In Gainesville stands the comfortable Harwood-Gibbs house, built in antebellum days when Gainesville thrived as a cotton port.

161

Marion

The King-Barron-Arbuthnot House

Giant camellia bushes and boxwood surround this gleaming white mansion — Marion's finest. Slender fluted columns give the front portico a spacious air that blends well with the delicate grillwork of the balcony. Porter King, who built the house in 1849, was the Confederate officer to whom General Bee at the first Battle of Manassas made the remark about General Thomas J. Jackson "standing like a stone wall." From this time on Jackson was known as "Stonewall Jackson." Dr. William Barron purchased the King estate in 1906, and his daughter Mrs. Joseph W. Arbuthnot occupies the house today.

The Lea-Stewart-Thatcher House

One of the most famous marriages in Alabama occurred in this house. After a whirlwind courtship Sam Houston in 1840 married Margaret Moffette Lea in spite of the opposition of her family and his friends. The Lea family lived here until 1917 when Arthur Stewart purchased the house. His daughter Mrs. Gray Thatcher and her family reside in the house today.

Eutaw

The Herndon-Alexander-Webb House

Typical of Eutaw's many antebellum mansions with wide verandas is this house on Main street. In spite of the need for repair evident in this picture, made during the depression of the 1930's, the house retains an ageless charm. Thomas H. Herndon bought the house in 1850 after it was moved from Erie. When the Herndons moved to Mobile, Mrs. Herndon's sister and her husband, Dr. Henry Young Webb, acquired the house; it has been continuously occupied by their descendants. Van Gilder Webb has restored the old home.

This rear view before restoration reveals why it has been called the "Ruffled Front House" - a broad impressive front and a narrow unpretentious back.

Talladega

Talladega, one of the oldest settlements in Alabama, boasts many antebellum homes on its tree-shaded avenues and in its surrounding countryside. Pioneers moved here when it was on the boundary line between Cherokee and Creek lands, and from their log cabins came some of Talladega's most interesting homes.

Whitwood

In striking contrast to Talladega's many Greek Revival mansions is Whitwood, its arches suggestive of Spanish Colonial architecture. Built as a log cabin in 1835, it was later converted by the Pinckney Wood family.

Birmingham Chamber of Commerce

McClellan-Jones-McGehee House

In the midst of three thousand acres which he had purchased from the Creek Indians, General William E. McClellan built between 1830-1833 his brick Colonial home called Idlewilde. His daughter Idora McClellan, who became the well-known author and dialect reader Betsy Hamilton, spent her girlhood here. The stage road to Rome, Georgia, passed in front of the house.

Wetumpka

Kelly Fitzpatrick House

In spite of the dilapidation shown in this old picture, this house of Alabama's famed artist manages to retain the dignity and charm that once marked it as a show place of Wetumpka. Formerly it was surrounded by well-kept grounds with ancient trees and brick walks leading through the garden. The house was razed in the 1950's.

Montgomery

As the capital in the era of Alabama's greatest prosperity before the Civil War, Montgomery had many fine residences. Most of these houses were erected near the river front in what is now the business section of the city and were demolished to make way for commercial property. The few which have survived are used mostly for business purposes today.

Photo by John Scott

The Falconer House

A giant wisteria vine entwines the porch of this cottage on Perry street, built in 1845 by John Falconer. In 1818 on the stagecoach from Milledgeville to Montgomery Falconer met Andrew Dexter who persuaded him to help finance the plan to build a town at the big bend of the Alabama river.

166

The Bibb House

A poignant reminder of the past, the Bibb house stood surrounded by businesses until it was razed in 1967. Benajah Smith Bibb, brother of Governors William Wyatt and Thomas Bibb, built the house in 1832.

Family heirlooms filled the spacious rooms of the old Bibb house. The mantel portrait of a baby with only one shoe pictures Dr. William George Bibb at eighteen months. Dr. Bibb's daughter, Mrs. Mattie Bibb Edmondson, occupied the house until it was demolished.

Sophia Gilmer Bibb

Mrs. Bibb, wife of Benajah Smith Bibb, was a distinguished Montgomery social and civic leader. During the Civil War she rendered notable service as a nurse. Later she founded the Ladies Memorial Association and for twenty-one years served as its president. Under her leadership the graves of hundreds of Confederate soldiers were marked, and the Confederate Monument was erected on the capitol grounds. This portrait hangs in the Alabama Department of Archives and History.

Photo by John Scott

The Owens-Teague House

Architects consider this brick house with its marble portico one of the finest Greek Revival mansions in the South. Berry Owens, a prosperous livery stable operator, built the house in 1848. From the balcony General Wilson read President Lincoln's Emancipation Proclamation to a throng of Negroes.

Stanley Paulger Studios

Mansions such as this Greek Revival edifice appeared along River street in Montgomery during the Golden Era of King Cotton. This picture of the Cowles-Goldthwaite house was made in 1874 before it was demolished.

Photo by Alex Bush

The Gilmer-Shorter-Lomax House

From this fashionable mansion went young Tennant Lomax in 1861 to the battle fields of Virginia. He was killed one year later during the Battle of Seven Pines. This Greek Revival house was built in 1848 on lot number one of the settlement from which Montgomery grew. Today it is headquarters for an insurance company.

The Murphy House

This picture made in the early 1930's shows the fate of many antebellum mansions in Alabama. The John Murphy house at the corner of Bibb and Coosa streets stood in the midst of spacious grounds when it was built in 1852. Now in the center of downtown Montgomery, it serves as an Elk's Club.

HABS, Library of Congress

169

The White House of the Confederacy

This simple spacious house was the Montgomery home of Jefferson Davis and his family during their brief stay in the city. The white frame house with green shutters was built about 1852 by William Sayre; A. M. Bradley was the architect. Of unusual interest are the liberty cap ventilators.

Around this gleaming mahogany table President and Mrs. Davis entertained important personages in the dining room of the White House. The corner cupboard houses a tea set of the Moss Rose pattern used by the Davises at Beauvoir, and on the sideboard is the silver service Mrs. Davis used while living in the White House.

170

Shown here are the two parlors in the White House. The rosewood chairs
are from the home of William Rufus King, a former vice-president of the
United States. The cornices over the windows are imported brass pieces from
the Davis plantation home at Brierfield, Mississippi. On the table in the
center foreground rests the Davis's family Bible. It was taken from Brierfield
during the war by a Federal soldier and was returned many years later to the
White House by his younger brother. The portrait over the mantel is of
Varina Howell Davis. The other portrait is of the Polish artist, Nicola Marschall, who designed not only the Confederacy's Stars and Bars but also the
Confederate uniform.

In the spacious entrance hall many important guests were received during the
five months that the Confederate government was located in Montgomery.
Note the marble-topped console table wtih petticoat mirror underneath. The
grandfather clock was made by John Hagey of Germantown, Pennsylvania, in
1810. In the rear may be seen the Jefferson Davis shrine with Davis's portrait
and the Confederate flag.

CHANTILLY

The plantation house called Chantilly was one of several such houses built at Mt. Meigs, a lively social and political centre in antebellum Alabama. Among the first of several South Carolinians to seek a cotton fortune in this fertile Black Belt country was young Dr. Thomas Burge Taylor, a graduate of Jefferson Medical College in Philadelphia. He married Harriott Pinckney Raoul of an aristocratic Charleston family. In 1832 as a wedding gift for his bride, Dr. Taylor purchased a plantation home which Harriott, of French ancestry, named Chantilly for Napoleon's summer home.

Possessing the Charlestonian love of gardens, the young Mrs. Taylor, aided by a French gardener brought from Charleston, set about to beautify the grounds of Chantilly. The lawn in front of the house was terraced, and summer houses were placed on either side of the circular drive. Twin magnolias, one of which is still standing, were planted at the front entrance while crepe myrtles and cherry laurels were clipped into intricate designs. At the rear were rose gardens with neat walks bordered by daily roses. Roman hyacinth, narcissus, and daffodil carpeted the lawn in the spring.

Architecturally Chantilly belongs to a style called "Southern Planter." Similar to the so-called grand mansions in many ways, this house is distinctively simple and is marked by an unflaunted dignity. Long and rangy, it is fronted by a gallery or piazza extending part way around two sides of the house. Columnettes support the low roof with its dormer window. Dr. Taylor added two large rooms on either side of the back of the house forming the ideal T-shape popular in the grand mansions.

Slave labor built Chantilly from hand-hewn timbers put together with pegs. The foundation rests on bricks made on the plantation, the wooden molds for which may be seen today. From Mobile came hardware for the doors—heavy English locks and silver keyholes with covers. The Taylors furnished their home with fine pieces, many of them family heirlooms from South Carolina. Paintings, music, and books played an important part in the cultured atmosphere of Chantilly, and Dr. Taylor provided his family with sheet music for the Chickering piano, with magazines and books, and many fine paintings, including several by Thomas Sully.

All: Courtesy of Mrs. Florence Charles Hall. Photos by Paul Robertson

Dr. Taylor owned three plantations but Chantilly was known as the home-place. Here cotton and wool were spun and woven into cloth. Here leather was tanned and cider was made. Here slaves needing medical attention were treated and hospitalized. Harriott Taylor not only trained slaves as house servants but directed them in the making of candles, preserving of meats, drying of fruits, and even the cutting and sizing of shoes.

Dr. and Mrs. Taylor had no children, but his sister Frances, after her marriage to Robert Frazier Charles, made Chantilly her home, and her son William Charles inherited the house from Dr. Taylor. Today a sixth-generation heir of Dr. Taylor's, Mrs. Florence Charles Hall, occupies Chantilly and has preserved it as a showplace of plantation life.

Dominating the parlor is the unusually fine portrait of young William Charles and his sister Mary, painted in 1849 by J. Winterhalter, brother of the famed German artist Franz Zavier Winterhalter. J. Winterhalter, who was working his way across the United States, stopped at Mt. Meigs long enough to paint the Charles children. The coffee table in front of the Empire sofa was made from the buckboard of the buggy in which the Taylor family came to Alabama. For years this seat was used in the outside kitchen for the cook's children to sit on. At the end of the Victorian sofa is a tatting table designed to hold needlework.

(Continued)

The entrance into the dining room may have once been the front door of the house before it was enlarged. The side-light panes are of Belgium glass, brilliantly colored in reds, blues, and pink.

The dining room is filled with family heirlooms. A family Bible stands open in front of the fireplace with its original Adam's mantel. The pastel portraits above the mantel of Dr. Taylor and his wife, first owners of Chantilly, were done by their niece Carolyn Theus Raoul. The Empire sideboard was brought by Mrs. Taylor from South Carolina when she came to Alabama in 1832. In the "mammy rocker" many Charles babies were lulled to sleep.

Lowndesboro

The Thomas-Hagood-Meadows House

Both: Selma Times Journal

The thirteen columns rising to the roof on two sides of this white frame mansion give it a striking appearance. The builder added elaborate brackets and iron lace balconies to enhance the beauty of Meadowlawn, a name given this antebellum home by Random Meadows after the Civil War.

The Powell-Steele House

Lorenzo Powell purchased in 1818 the land on which he built his homestead. The house is distinguished by four outside brick chimneys and stands in sturdy contrast to its more elegant neighbors.

The Tyson-Randolph House

When Archibald Tyson built his home in Lowndesboro, he desired, as did so many other planters in the 1850's, to build for comfort as well as beauty. As protection against the hot summer sun he built the Pillars in the shape of an L so that each room in the house would have cross ventilation. For beauty he added two major porticoes, one with six Doric columns and the other with four.

Much rocking, resting, and visiting was done on this comfortable porch, as evidenced by this picture made before restoration.

Selma

Selma stands on a high bluff on the north bank of the Alabama river. Buildings with lacy iron balconies and shady streets with white-columned houses give the town an antebellum air. In the flush years Selma became the center of the Black Belt domain of King Cotton. Many lawyers settled in and around Selma to enjoy its prosperity. Horse racing and cock fighting flourished on a scale unknown in the rest of the state. In this setting some of the finest houses in the state were built. In spite of the destruction in Selma by Federal troops at the close of the Civil War, many of these homes stand today.

Selma and Dallas County Chamber of Commerce

The Mabry-Jones House

Strikingly different from the wooden houses surrounding it on Tremont street is the red-brick Mabry home. Dr. Albert Gallatin Mabry, who was instrumental in organizing the state medical association, built the home in 1850 and his great-grandson Catesby ap Roger Jones lives here today. Dr. Mabry's step-daughter Gertrude Tartt married the Confederate naval officer Captain Catesby ap Roger Jones who was in charge of the Selma Ordnance Works during the Civil War. They occupied the house until the death of Captain Jones in 1878.

The Welch House

This house occupied by the Misses Kate and Bessie Welch has sometimes been referred to as the White House of Baptist ministers because so many clerics of that denomination have stayed here. The two-story wooden structure, surmounted by a cupola, was built in 1858 by William B. King and was sold to William Pressley Welch in 1887.

The Oaks

In 1850 Kirkland Harrison, a lover of horse racing and good living, built the Oaks on the road from Cahawba to Summerfield. The house dominates a grove of oaks and was once part of a large plantation. Judge John Starke Hunter bought the house in 1853, and it remained in his family until about 1900. The present owners, Mr. and Mrs. Kenneth M. Harper, have carefully restored and preserved the property.

HABS, Library of Congress

These wooden hand-carved doors once graced the governor's mansion at Cahawba. As Cahawba became increasingly vulnerable to flooding, the house was dismantled and moved to Tremont street in Selma. Here it became the home of Colonel and Mrs. N. H. R. Dawson, a half-sister of Mrs. Abraham Lincoln. In the 1960's the Dawson home was razed, but these unusual doors appear on the house built on the site where once stood the Dawson home.

STURDIVANT HALL

Edward T. Watts, one of Selma's most prosperous cotton planters, commissioned Thomas Helm Lee, architect-cousin of Robert E. Lee, to build this fine Greek Revival mansion. The house had cost Watts $69,000 by the time it was completed in 1853. It was sold in 1863 for $65,000 to John M. Parkman, a successful banker, who met a tragic death after the Civil War attempting to escape from the Federal prison at Cahawba. In 1870 Emile Gillman, a German who came to Selma to bake bread for the Confederate army, bought the house for $12,000. It remained in the Gillman family until the city of Selma purchased the property in 1952. Most of the money for this purchase came from the estate of Robert Daniel Sturdivant, who had left $50,000 for a museum. Sturdivant Hall stands today restored to its former splendor.

179

(Continued)

One of the many features which this house has in common with Stanton Hall at Natchez is the side entrance with ornamental iron decoration.

The small parlor combines expert architectural detailing with elegant furnishings: a Charleston tilt tea table, a Chippendale side chair, and an elaborate gold leaf mirror. Over the Hepplewhite sofa hangs a portrait of Frederick Ravesies, land agent for the Vine and Olive Colony. This painting was given to Sturdivant Hall by Ravesies' granddaughter, a resident of Selma.

In the courtyard at the rear of the house is the original kitchen with its open fireplace and Dutch oven for cooking. The pine table holds old kitchen utensils: a coffee mill, wooden bread tray, mortar and pestle, and a sausage stuffer.

The distinctive framings of the doors, used throughout the house, and the checkered pattern of the marble floor make for an interesting hall. The Jacobean chest and the Italian side chair came from the New York studio of Selma artist Clara Weaver Parrish.

Camden

White Columns

On the Alabama river cotton planter Felix Tait, son of James Asbury Tait, built his home. He began its construction in 1859 and finished it just before he left to serve in the Civil War. The Tait family lived at White Columns until 1880 when Dr. Lucius Ernest Starr purchased it, and his descendants occupy the house now. The unusual twin white-columned porticoes dominate this eighteen room mansion. It contains many fine antiques, including prize J.M.W. Turner engravings.

Courtesy of Kathryn Tucker Windham

The King Plantation House

William Rufus King chose Black's Bend in the Alabama river for his homesite, but his nephew, William T. King, continued down the Alabama to Packer's Bend to build on one of the largest plantation acreages in the area. William T. King inherited from his uncle sixty-five slaves, some of them trained builders. Their skill is evident in this beautiful mansion begun in the 1850's but never completed on the scale that it was first conceived. The home has identical upper and lower floors with twin parlors and verandas on both levels. This large house with its sixteen fireplaces has retained its magnificent dignity in spite of the ravages of time seen in this picture. In the 1960's the house was moved to Euriah, but at the river landing below where King's slaves once loaded cotton the old warehouse, commissary, and gin still stand.

Clarke County Democrat

Standing proudly on its 160 acres of plantation land, the aristocratic James S. Dickinson home, built in the 1840's, has dominated the Grove Hill scene for over a hundred years. Particularly exquisite is the arched front door with its intricate wood carving and colored glass fan and side lights.

Mobile

The fascinating story of Alabama's oldest city is told in its architecture in which French, Spanish, English, and American influences combine to give it a distinctive flavor. Here were the original French Colonial houses, and here the raised cottage type, designed to escape floods, was born. Particularly characteristic of Mobile is the ornamental ironwork first imported from France in the 1780's. Later, delicate patterns of wrought iron, forged by hand, were made by local craftsmen, most of them Negro slaves. About 1830 heavy cast-iron designs came from Philadelphia to Mobile in sailing ships. The earlier wrought ironwork with its simplicity of line and ribbon-like character is considered more valuable today.

Photo by Victor Haagen

The Kirkbride House

This house is one of Alabama's most historic landmarks. The foundation of the building is believed to be part of Fort Conde de la Mobile, built by the French in 1770. Mobile's first courthouse and jail were housed here. Jonathan Kirkbride purchased the house in 1885 and converted it into a residence. Four massive Tuscan columns support the balcony while the roof is supported by ornate Corinthian columns. The house is constructed of brick covered with stucco, painted white.

The Admiral Semmes House

In the hard times around 1871 Mobilians raised money to buy this house for Admiral Raphael Semmes, and here he spent the last years of his life. Built in the 1850's by Peter Horta, the house still emanates charm and appeal.

Sometimes called "frozen lace," iron grillwork gives the simplest house an air of elegance.

Delaney, Remember Mobile

The plaster work at the Yester house is second only to that at Gaineswood. Dumb waiters from the basement kitchen brought food to the dining room.

The Yester House

An avenue of superb oak trees leads up to this homestead in Spring Hill, built in 1840 by cotton merchant William Dawson. A sunken garden and arrangements of formal shrubs were once part of the landscaping. Dawson used Carolina marble, plaster from Italy, and hard-pine timber in the house which, it is said, cost fifty thousand dollars.

OAKLEIGH

Oakleigh stands upon the highest point of what was known as Simon Fabre's old Spanish Land Grant. It receives its name from the many beautiful giant oaks surrounding it. James W. Roper, serving as his own architect and builder, started this house in 1833 and completed it by 1838 when he brought his bride here to live. The curved stair leading from the porch to the lower floor is a masterpiece. A leading Mobile architect has said, "Perhaps Oakleigh's outstanding quality is its individuality . . . It has the quiet charm of the best of the Louisiana plantation homes but it is a different charm; in fact Oakleigh is Oakleigh." Today Oakleigh is headquarters for the Historic Mobile Preservation Society.

Preserved in the double parlors are treasures from demolished Mobile homes. Marble mantels in both parlors came from the Hatter house and the gold leaf mirrors over the mantels from the Emanuel house. In the foreground is an early nineteenth century English supper table on which is displayed an Old Paris china service. The silk brocaded curtains made in France in 1856 were put together with strands of spun gold.

The Staples House

This house, built about 1840, is probably the largest Creole cottage in the South and certainly in the Mobile area. Norman A. Staples purchased the cottage in 1901, and his granddaughter Mary Buff Kimbrough Bancroft in the 1960's has restored this unusual house to its original condition. The section in which the Staples place is located was known as Summerville in antebellum days because so many Mobilians erected fashionable summer homes along Old Shell road. This road derived its name from shells taken from Mobile Bay and used for a roadbed.

The Staples house with its simple grace is typical of Creole architecture. The high gabled roof, framed to include the veranda as well as the rest of the house, keeps the glare of the summer sun from the rooms within. The dormer windows both front and back are framed by blinds useful as well as decorative.

In the grove Spanish moss hangs from giant oaks estimated to be over three hundred years old.

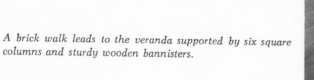

A brick walk leads to the veranda supported by six square columns and sturdy wooden bannisters.

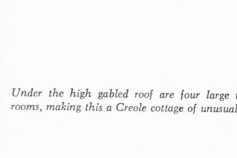

Under the high gabled roof are four large upstairs bedrooms, making this a Creole cottage of unusual proportions.

BELLINGRATH

The garden which Mr. and Mrs. Walter D. Bellingrath began to develop almost fifty years ago at their fishing camp near Mobile has become one of the great gardens of America. Beginning with a few azaleas planted around the camp lodge among moss-covered oaks and magnolias, the Bellingraths gradually added more flowering plants and shrubs. They eventually had fifty-five acres landscaped under the supervision of the well-known Southern architect, George B. Rogers. Much of the planting was done by Mrs. Bellingrath, who wanted each tree, vine, and plant to be left undisturbed in its natural setting.

This picturesque spot on a bluff overlooking the Isle-aux-Oise river presents a colorful panorama of blooming flowers all seasons of the year, but with azaleas in bloom Bellingrath comes into its full glory. There are more than 250,000 azalea plants ranging from dwarf Kurume to the giant plants of the Indica varieties, some eighteen feet in height. Many of these magnificent plants are more than 150 years old. The gardens also contain more than four thousand specimens of Camellia Japonica and Camellia Sasanqua.

Complementing the gardens is the Bellingrath house, beautiful enough in itself to be the focal point of the estate. In 1925 the architect Rogers designed and built for the Bellingraths a two-story mansion, a blending of French, Spanish, and English influences. The house is centered around a patio set against a background of handmade brick colonnades and lacy ironwork from old Mobile buildings.

For many years Bessie Morse Bellingrath, a discriminating collector, filled her house with priceless silver, china, glassware, and furniture. Much of the furnishings came from the estate of Baroness Micaela Pontalba of New Orleans. Today these treasures are displayed in the settings for which Mrs. Bellingrath selected them. Recently the Bellingrath gardens have acquired a magnificent collection of Boehm porcelain birds, ranging in size from a few inches to a seven-foot ivory billed woodpecker.

Although it was developed in the 1900's, Bellingrath is included with antebellum homes of Mobile because of its colonial architecture and antique furnishings.

Both: Courtesy of Bellingrath Gardens. Photos by Fred W. Holder

The patio with its antique grillwork captures the charm of old Mobile. In colonial days on land which the gardens now occupy Spanish grandees bred champion bulls for the bullrings in Madrid.

ısed in this sprawling mansion are many fine collections. In
Bottle Room, set among shelves of Venetian, Waterford, and
er fine glass, is a plain, sturdy bottle, one of the earliest types
l for Coca-Cola, the soft drink that led to the foundation of
Bellingrath's fortune.

191

(Continued)

All: Courtesy of Bellingrath Gardens. Photos by Fred W. Holder

Over the dining room's Adam mantel is a fine oval mirror in gilt filigree.

The dining room is one of the most impressive rooms in the South. Covering the floor is a two-hundred-year-old gold pattern Aubusson rug. The enormous Chippendale dining table and its sixteen chairs were formerly owned by Sir Thomas Lipton, the English tea magnate and yachting enthusiast. On the table is a Dresden centerpiece of figurines.

The twin beds in the upstairs guest room are Sheraton pieces. The slipper sofas are Empire style.

The drawing room with its delicately proportioned staircase is elegantly furnished in the Late Victorian manner with Louis XVI chairs and mirror, Dresden and Meissen porcelains, and antique satin brocaded draperies and upholstering.

The Bragg-Mitchell House

Thousands of visitors annually follow the flower-lined Azalea Trail that winds past this home, pictured here with azaleas in full bloom along its semi-circular driveway. When Judge John Bragg completed his term in the United States Senate in 1854, he hired Mobile's best architect, Thomas S. James, to design this gracious Greek Revival mansion. The sixteen slender columns set around the three-sided veranda are a striking departure from the usual massive columns of this type. During the Civil War Confederate artillery men cut the old trees on the homesite to give freer range for shelling approaching Federal troops. After the war Judge Bragg planted the acorns that grew into these live oaks shown here.

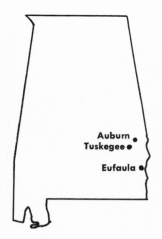

The Chattahoochee River Area

Tuskegee

The Varner-Alexander House

William Varner, a wealthy Black Belt planter of Macon county, designed and supervised construction of this elegant Greek Revival mansion in Tuskegee. This architectural drawing made for the Historic American Buildings Survey emphasized the Doric columns, the lavishly designed window cornices, and the delicately wrought iron grill on the balcony. The octagonal cupola dominates this fine old brick mansion. During the Civil War the house was saved from destruction when the commander of the Federal troops recognized Mr. Varner as a classmate at Harvard and ordered his men to spare it.

195

Auburn

Photo by George M

The Halliday-Cary-Pick House

Few antebellum houses remain in Auburn. A notable exception is this home recognized by the Historic American Buildings Survey as having outstanding architectural merit. Built in 1852, it served as a hospital in the Civil War. Dr. C. A. Cary, founder of Auburn University's School of Veterinary Medicine, bought the house in 1890. General Lewis A. Pick, famous as the builder of the Ledo road in Burma during World War II, married Dr. Cary's daughter and lived here until his death in 1956. Dr. Cary's daughter occupies the house today.

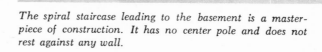

DEPARTMENT OF THE INTERIOR
WASHINGTON · D · C ·
THIS · IS · TO · CERTIFY · THAT · THE ·
HISTORIC · BUILDING ·
· KNOWN · AS ·
· HOLLIDAY · CARY · HOME ·
· IN · THE · COUNTY · OF ·
· LEE ·
· AND · THE · STATE · OF ·
· ALABAMA ·
· HAS · BEEN · SELECTED · BY · THE ·
· ADVISORY · COMMITTEE · OF · THE ·
HISTORIC · AMERICAN ·
BUILDINGS · SURVEY ·
· AS · POSSESSING · EXCEPTIONAL ·
· HISTORIC · OR · ARCHITECTURAL ·
· INTEREST · AND · AS · BEING · WORTHY ·
· OF · MOST · CAREFUL · PRESERVATION ·
· FOR · THE · BENEFIT · OF · FUTURE ·
· GENERATIONS · AND · THAT · TO · THIS ·
· END · A · RECORD · OF · ITS · PRESENT ·
· APPEARANCE · AND · CONDITION ·
· HAS · BEEN · MADE · AND · DEPOSITED ·
· FOR · PERMANENT · REFERENCE · IN · THE ·
LIBRARY · OF · CONGRESS ·

· ATTEST ·

Ter Burkhardt
· District · Officer ·

Harold L. Ickes
· Secretary · of · the · Interior ·

The spiral staircase leading to the basement is a masterpiece of construction. It has no center pole and does not rest against any wall.

Not all cotton planters lived in grand mansions. Houses such as this one, built in 1834 near Clayton by Matthew Fenn, were a common sight throughout Alabama.

197

Eufaula

On a high bluff overlooking the Chattahoochee river and the Georgia lowlands, this old river town is the setting for some of Alabama's finest and best-preserved antebellum houses. During the cotton boom Eufaula became the port city for cotton grown in eastern Alabama; steamboats and barges, loading bales for shipment to New York and England, crowded the river landings. Wealthy planters lined the tree-shaded streets with their impressive houses, many of them topped with a cupola. Eufaulians have carefully preserved these old mansions which stand today in tribute to a rich heritage.

The tavern is the Bluff City's link with old Irwinton, the little Indian village that was destined to become present Eufaula. Built by Edward Williams in about 1836, this historic landmark has served as an inn to accommodate stage and river traffic, a Confederate hospital, and a residence. Today this house on the bluff is beautifully restored and is once again a focal point for the town.

Traceable through the shadows in this picture is the old road bed winding down to the wharf on the Chattahoochee.

The Kendall-Eppes House

Rising majestically on a hillside is Kendall Manor, considered by many to be the finest example of the Italianate style in Alabama. The cupola is the crowning touch to this architectural masterpiece which was built by James Turner Kendall for his Scottish bride, Mary Jane McRae. Construction on the house was begun before the Civil War with slave labor, but it was not completed until the war was over. Former slaves returned to help complete the building. Five generations of the Kendalls have lived here, and nine Kendall brides have walked down the beautiful stairway to be married in the back parlor.

The Cato House

In a town noted for its cupolas, the Cato mansion claims one of unusual interest; the cupola is almost a replica of the main house. Lewis Llewellen Cato, who had come from Georgia to practice law in Eufaula, built this house in 1858 on land purchased from the Creek Indians. When Alabama seceded from the Union, Cato, an ardent secessionist and friend of Yancey's, staged a great celebration in this house.

Lavish furnishings adorn the parlor in Dean Hall—elegant reminders of the days of cotton glory in Eufaula.

The Bray-Barron House

New Englander Nathan Bray defied the Greek Revival tradition when he built this charming cottage-type house with its square columns. The house has been recently restored, and beautiful antique furnishings belonging to the present owners, the N. G. Barrons, make it a showplace.

The Confederate monument
stood in Huntsville's courthouse square until 1965.

CSA

1861-1865

IN MEMORY OF
THE HEROES WHO FELL
IN DEFENCE OF THE
PRINCIPLES WHICH
GAVE B...TY TO THE
CONFEDE...TE C...SE

EREC...
DAUGHT...

THE CIVIL WAR

Harper's Weekly

Drumming up recruits for the Confederate army in front of the Exchange Hotel, Montgomery, Alabama

YANCEY LEADS THE SOUTH TO SECESSION

Alabamians studied national events throughout the 1850's with growing apprehension. Such apprehension was shared by the state's major political figures, William Lowndes Yancey, Democrat, and Henry Washington Hilliard, acknowledged head of the Whig party. Yancey in particular was an avid "states' rights" advocate. With passionate oratory and lurid newspaper prose, Yancey attacked those who threatened "states' rights." More than a decade before the Civil War Yancey led in authoring the Alabama Platform, a declaration which stated that Congress had no right to prevent slaveholders from taking their slaves into any territory. Congress should also provide protection for "slave property" in such territories. The Democrats of Alabama in their state convention in 1848 approved this Alabama Platform.

Important events of the 1850's strengthened Yancey's position in the South. There was Bleeding Kansas, the North's reaction to the Dred Scott Decision, and nullification of the Fugitive Slave Act by the Northern states. John Brown's raid at Harper's Ferry convinced many Alabamians of rumors that Northern abolitionists were sending money and organizers among the Southern slaves to precipitate their rebellion. Promptly after the Harper's Ferry raid the Alabama legislature provided two hundred thousand dollars to outfit eight thousand volunteer troops for protection. As part of this provision two young men from each county in the state went to La Grange or Glenville military academies for officer training.

In the 1850's Yancey worked closely with Edmund Ruffin of Virginia and Robert Barnwell Rhett of South Carolina to help form the Southern Rights Associations. By 1858 Yancey was creating Leagues of United Southerners. While Yancey was expressing such sentiments, extremists in the North were expressing equally belligerent views.

Alabama's support for Yancey's secessionist program increased rapidly as the 1860's approached and with it harsher feelings North

William Lowndes Yancey
"The fiery orator of secession," hailed as the greatest speaker since Patrick Henry

and South. The political machinery in Alabama was in the hands of ardent secessionists, among them the governor of the state, A. B. Moore. Only north Alabama and the Wiregrass region boasted a large vocal segment that rejected secession, and this group was more vocal than politically powerful in the state.

When the Democratic convention of 1860 met in Charleston, South Carolina, the Alabama delegates were instructed to place before this convention the famed Alabama Platform earlier presented to and accepted by the Alabama Democratic Convention of 1848. This time on a national scale the Democratic convention refused the Alabama Platform, and William L. Yancey led his Alabama cohorts from the convention hall. A number of delegates from other Southern states followed, and Yancey's maneuver forced the convention to adjourn without nominating a presidential and vice-presi-

Summersell, Alabama History

HARPER'S WEEKLY *in an issue of January, 1861, illustrated the coming secession convention with this drawing.*

dential candidate. Later, delegates from Northern states held their own private meeting and nominated Stephen A. Douglas of Illinois as Democratic candidate for president in 1860. Delegates from Southern states responded by holding their own private convention and nominating John C. Breckinridge of Kentucky. Yancey left this Southern convention to organize the Southern Democratic Party and to make more than one hundred speeches for Breckinridge from New Orleans to New York. Meanwhile, in the mid-South the Constitutional Union nominated John Bell of Tennessee for president. As a result of various caucuses, conventions, and nominations splintering the Democratic Party in 1860, friends of Breckinridge, Douglas, and Bell were very active in Alabama during all of the campaign. Republican presidential nominee, lanky Abe Lincoln, popular in the North, had no organized support in Alabama. In fact,

Henry W. Hilliard
This brilliant minister, lawyer, and educator held his own in debates with Yancey.

(Continued)

Montgomery Advertiser:
EXTRA.

Saturday Morning, January 12, 1861.

The Act of Secession.

Yesterday, at about the hour of half-past two, P. M., the following Ordinance, withdrawing Alabama from the Union, was adopted in the State Convention by a vote of 61 ayes to 39 noes, and the President of the Convention pronounced Alabama a free, sovereign and independent State.

An Ordinance to dissolve the Union between the State of Alabama and other States united under the Compact Styled "the United States of America."

WHEREAS, the election of Abraham Lincoln and Hannibal Hamlin to the offices of President and Vice President of the United States of America, by a sectional party, avowedly hostile to the domestic institutions, and to the peace and security of the people of the State of Alabama, following upon the heels of many, and dangerous infractions of the Constitution of the United States by many of the States, and people of the Northern section, is a political wrong of so insulting and menacing character as to justify the people of the State of Alabama in the adoption of prompt and decided measures for their future peace and security.

Therefore, *Be it declared and ordained by the people of the State of Alabama, in Convention assembled*, That the State of Alabama now withdraws, and is hereby withdrawn from the Union, known as "the United States of America," and henceforth ceases to be one of said United States, and is, and of right ought to be a sovereign and independent State.

SEC. 2. *And be it further declared and ordained by the people of the State Alabama in Convention assembled*, That all the powers over the Territory of said State, and over the people thereof, heretofore delegated to the Government of the United States of America, be and they are hereby withdrawn from said Government, and are hereby resumed and vested in the people of the State of Alabama.

And as it is the desire and purpose of the people of Alabama to meet the slaveholding States of the South, who may approve such purpose, in order to frame a provisional as well as permanent Government upon the principles of the Constitution of the United States.

Be it also Resolved by the people of Alabama in Convention assembled, That the people of the States of Delaware, Maryland, Virginia, North Carolina, South Carolina, Florida, Georgia, Mississippi, Louisiana, Texas, Arkansas, Tennessee, Kentucky and Missouri, be and are hereby invited to meet the people of the State of Alabama by their Delegates, in Convention, on the 4th day of February, A. D., 1861, at the City of Montgomery, in the State of Alabama, for the purpose of consulting with each other as to the most effectual mode of securing concerted and harmonious action in whatever measures may be deemed most desirable for our common peace and security.

And be it further Resolved, That the President of this Convention, be and is hereby instructed to transmit forthwith a copy of the foregoing preamble, ordinance, and resolutions to the Governors of the several States named in said resolutions.

Done by the people of the State of Alabama, in Convention assembled, at Montgomery, on this the eleventh day of January, A. D., 1861.

The Act of Secession comprised the entire issue of the MONTGOMERY ADVERTISER for January 12, 1861. It announced the withdrawing of Alabama from the Union and declared her to be "a free, sovereign and independent state."

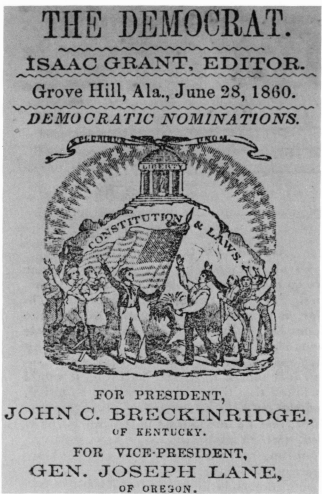

Clarke County Democrat, January 10, 1861

throughout Alabama and the South, Breckinridge supporters agreed that the South must leave the Union if Lincoln became president. After Lincoln won the election, the burning question everywhere was whether or not the political Southern leaders would make good their secession threat.

The answer came soon. Lincoln won the election on November 6, 1860. Six weeks later, December 20, South Carolina seceded. Two weeks after this on January 7, 1861, the Alabama legislature reconvened in Montgomery. Thus far the Alabama legislature was making good its threat, because in February of 1860 it had resolved that the governor of Alabama should call a convention to consider the question of secession if a Republican won the presidential election.

As indicated by action from their elected officials, a large percentage of Alabamians favored withdrawing from the Union. Some favored immediate withdrawal, but the "cooperative secessionists" preferred waiting until other Southern states withdrew with Alabama. The cooperative secessionists also wanted to wait and see if Alabama could live with the new president. In general, the demand for immediate secession was strongest in central and south Alabama. North Alabama advocated delay. With fewer wealthy plantations, it was more closely attached to Tennessee in economics and geography than to central and south Alabama. Thus, as Tennesseans waited to study the secession question, north Alabama wanted to follow their example. Central and south Alabama won. After only four days of heated discussion, Alabama's "secession convention" followed her sister state of South Carolina and voted to secede on January 11, 1861.

As news of secession spread, crowds cheered, cannons boomed, and Alabama flags replaced the flags of the United States on most buildings. Only Tennessee valley groups showed apathy. Many north Alabama political leaders had de-

manded until the last that the decision for secession be submitted to popular vote throughout the state; now, with secession, there were loud demands in north Alabama for a "State of Nickajack" comprised of north Alabama counties adjacent to Tennessee and Georgia. The flag of the United States flew over the courthouses in Athens and Huntsville for several days after Alabama itself on January 11, 1861, had officially departed the Union.

Secession was one thing, however, and war another. Few in Alabama wanted fighting. It was generally believed and hoped that the North would not try to force the Southern states to remain in the Union. But unlikely and unwanted as such possibilities were, Alabama prepared for combat. Volunteers drilled in many counties amid optimism that all this was unnecessary. The legislature met in special session and voted five million dollars for a defense it did not hope to use. The legislature instructed the governor to sell two million dollars in bonds to raise more money for defense, but until Fort Sumter the typical Alabamian could not believe that his Northern brother meant physical harm.

By February, Alabama political leaders had invited all Southern states to send delegates to Montgomery to organize the Confederate States of America. Within four days a provisional constitution was adopted, and on the fifth day the convention elected Jefferson Davis as president and Alexander H. Stephens as vice-president. For the two top positions the Confederacy had selected recognized conservatives, men who had shown reluctance to secede. Jefferson Davis had long urged delay. Alexander H. Stephens had opposed secession until it was a fact. These two men had one other idea in common besides their hesitancy to leave the Union; they believed the North would use force to keep the Southern states from seceding. Time too quickly would prove them right.

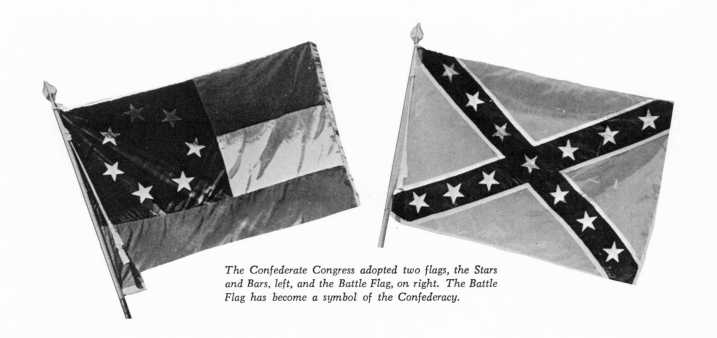

The Confederate Congress adopted two flags, the Stars and Bars, left, and the Battle Flag, on right. The Battle Flag has become a symbol of the Confederacy.

THE CONFEDERACY IS BORN

On February 4, 1861, in the state capitol in Montgomery delegates from all the seceding states organized the Confederate States of America. Normal activity stopped in Montgomery as groups gathered up and down Dexter avenue and around Court Square Fountain. Five days later the convention elected Jefferson Davis president, and Alexander H. Stephens vice-president.

Alabama's famous statesman and orator, William Lowndes Yancey, headed the reception committee that met President-elect Davis when he arrived in Montgomery for the inauguration. On the night of February 16 from the balcony of the Exchange Hotel, Yancey introduced Davis to the cheering crowd with words now famous: "The man and the hour have met."

The Confederacy inaugurated its president on Monday, February 18, 1861. Celebration of the event began early in the day. By midmorning a large crowd had gathered around the capitol. Then shortly before noon the parade began along Dexter avenue. First came the band, followed by the First Alabama Regiment and then a carriage, drawn by the traditional four white horses. In the carriage rode President-elect Jefferson Davis, Vice President-elect Alexander Stephens, a minister, and an army officer.

Only a week before Herman Arnold had orchestrated a tune called "Dixie." As Arnold led his musicians up the avenue, they began this tune never before played by a band. On this occasion it was called "I Wish I Was in Dixie's Land," the title under which it had been published the preceding June as sheet music arranged for piano. The music was stirring, the soldiers marched briskly, the horses pranced. As Mr. Davis's carriage passed, the crowd cheered and fell in behind the procession in its progress up the street toward the crowded capitol area. The carriage arrived at the capitol. The clock struck one. Howell Cobb administered the simple oath of office to Mr. Davis, who in turn made a brief inaugural speech. For the first and last time in its history, the South had installed a president of its own.

The inauguration of Jefferson Davis as president of the Confederacy at Montgomery, Alabama, was worldwide news. Reporters and artists covered it for European as well as United States papers. The above painting, five-by- *six feet, was made from a photograph taken on the spot and owned for many years by Colonel William C. Howell of Prattville, Alabama. It now hangs in the Alabama Department of Archives and History.*

209

Jefferson Davis
This portrait of Jefferson Davis made from a photograph taken while Davis was United States Secretary of War hangs in the White House of the Confederacy.

Varina Howell Davis
Eighteen years younger than her husband, Varina Howell Davis was a strikingly beautiful, dark-haired woman, a suitable subject for portraiture.

THE FIRST FAMILY

Jefferson Davis seemed to be an ideal man to head the Confederacy. He was a true Southerner, born in Kentucky and reared in Mississippi. A West Point graduate, he had distinguished himself as an officer in the Mexican War, and in 1853 Franklin Pierce had made him Secretary of War. Politically a strong supporter of state's rights, he typified the traditional Southern position. After the Pierce administration Davis became a Mississippi planter. In 1851 he lost a close race for the governorship of Mississippi, but in 1857 he was elected United States senator, a position he held until Mississippi seceded from the Union. As the war progressed Davis became involved in disagreements with some of the military members of his administration, and Lee's surrender at Appomattox was without his approval.

The devotion of Davis to his family was an inspiration in the turbulent war and reconstruction years. In 1845 he married Varina Howell of Mississippi, and they had two daughters and four sons. A marriage ten years earlier to the daughter of Zachary Taylor had ended after three months with her untimely death.

There was general Southern agreement that Davis and his family should live in a style comparable to that of the White House in Wash-

Harper's Weekly, June 1, 1861

The Congress of the Confederacy rented for the president's family this town house owned by Prattville cotton planter Edmund Harrison, and agreed to pay $5,000 a year.

ington. After Davis's inauguration on February 18, 1861, Varina Howell Davis with her children arrived from Mississippi on March 4 to take possession of the White House in Montgomery. On the same day Letitia Tyler raised the Confederacy's first flag on Capitol Hill. Alabamians crowded the city for this event as well as for the arrival of the First Lady. Music and admiring crowds greeted Mrs. Davis at the boat, and many admirers deluged the president's family with flowers.

The Congress of the Confederacy rented for the president's family the town house of Edmund Harrison, a Prattville cotton planter, and agreed to pay $5,000 a year.

When the Davis family moved into this house in 1861, it was located at the southwest corner of Bibb and Lee streets. Today this same building is on the corner of Union street and Washington avenue, immediately south of the State Capitol. The First White House Association, formed in 1900 to preserve the historic home, was responsible for the state's purchasing the building and for having it removed to state property in 1921.

The White House is a tourist attraction second only to the State Capitol. It is furnished in typical antebellum style and contains an interesting collection of Jefferson Davis's relics, which include many rare Confederate items.

Shown here is the Confederate Senate meeting at the capitol in Montgomery shortly after the firing on Fort Sumter. From this platform President Davis addressed the assembly with these words: "We feel that our cause is just and holy . . . All we ask is to be let alone; that those who never held power over us shall not now attempt our subjugation by arms. This we will, this we must, resist to the direst extremity."

THE CONFEDERATE GOVERNMENT
FORMS AT MONTGOMERY

A History of Montgomery in Pictures

An Alabamian, Robert T. Chapman, had the difficult task of bringing the Great Seal of the Confederacy from England, where it had been made, to the Confederate government in Richmond. Chapman, a nephew of Governor Reuben Chapman, successfully ran the Federal blockade, but in Bermuda part of the printing press was lost. Chapman delivered the seal to the Confederate authorities in Richmond, but it was never used.

212

Alabama Department of Archives and History

The original of this early sketch of Davis's cabinet is in the Library of Congress. It was made shortly after the government moved to Richmond. Here the cabinet confers with Robert E. Lee. LeRoy Pope Walker of Alabama, Secretary of War, is standing behind Jefferson Davis. Note the geographical diversity of this original cabinet: Stephen Mallory of Florida was Secretary of the Navy; Christopher Memminger of South Carolina was Secretary of the Treasury; John Reagan of Texas was Postmaster General; LeRoy Pope Walker of Alabama was Secretary of War; Robert Toombs of Georgia was Secretary of State; and Judah Benjamin of Louisiana was Attorney General.

LeRoy Pope Walker of Huntsville was recommended to President Jefferson Davis for Secretary of War by the die-hard secessionist William L. Yancey. Walker was offered his portfolio in the cabinet more from political expediency than from any deep conviction on the part of Jefferson Davis that he was fitted for the position. Because of ill health Walker resigned in September, 1861, after only seven months as a cabinet officer. Davis then made him a brigadier general in the Confederate army. After the war Walker headed the Alabama Constitutional Convention of 1875, as his father John Williams Walker had headed Alabama's first Constitutional Convention in 1819.

Both: Huntsville Times

Mrs. LeRoy Pope Walker before marriage to her famous husband was Eliza Dickson Pickett.

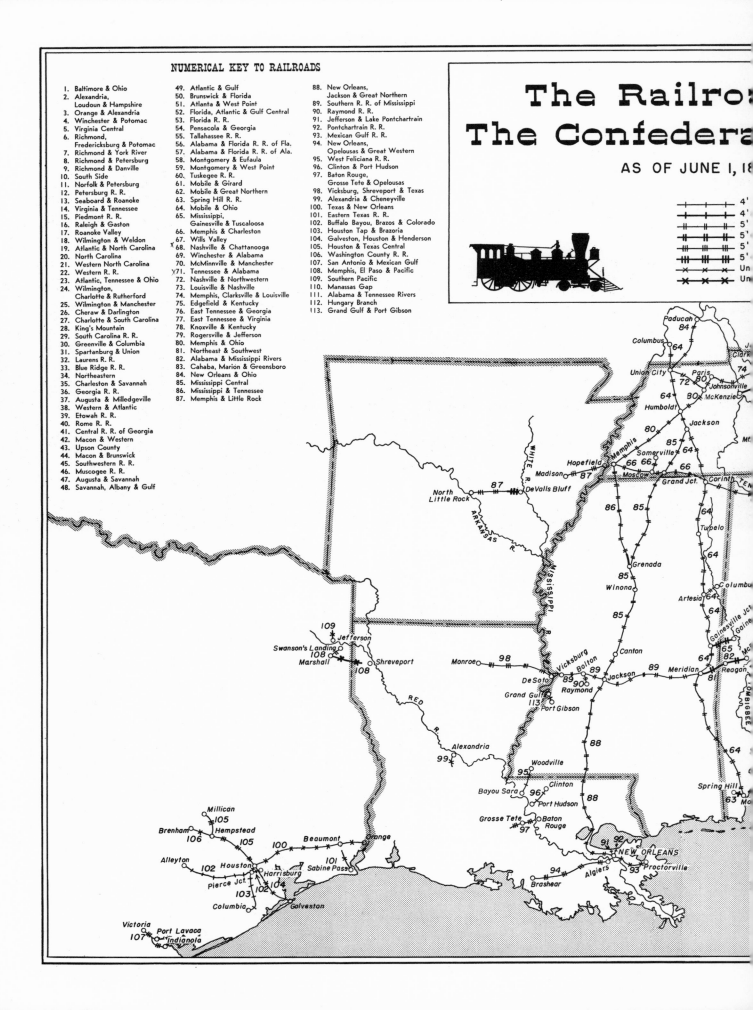

NUMERICAL KEY TO RAILROADS

1. Baltimore & Ohio
2. Alexandria, Loudoun & Hampshire
3. Orange & Alexandria
4. Winchester & Potomac
5. Virginia Central
6. Richmond, Fredericksburg & Potomac
7. Richmond & York River
8. Richmond & Petersburg
9. Richmond & Danville
10. South Side
11. Norfolk & Petersburg
12. Petersburg R. R.
13. Seaboard & Roanoke
14. Virginia & Tennessee
15. Piedmont R. R.
16. Raleigh & Gaston
17. Roanoke Valley
18. Wilmington & Weldon
19. Atlantic & North Carolina
20. North Carolina
21. Western North Carolina
22. Western R. R.
23. Atlantic, Tennessee & Ohio
24. Wilmington, Charlotte & Rutherford
25. Wilmington & Manchester
26. Cheraw & Darlington
27. Charlotte & South Carolina
28. King's Mountain
29. South Carolina R. R.
30. Greenville & Columbia
31. Spartanburg & Union
32. Laurens R. R.
33. Blue Ridge R. R.
34. Northeastern
35. Charleston & Savannah
36. Georgia R. R.
37. Augusta & Milledgeville
38. Western & Atlantic
39. Etowah R. R.
40. Rome R. R.
41. Central R. R. of Georgia
42. Macon & Western
43. Upson County
44. Macon & Brunswick
45. Southwestern R. R.
46. Muscogee R. R.
47. Augusta & Savannah
48. Savannah, Albany & Gulf

49. Atlantic & Gulf
50. Brunswick & Florida
51. Atlanta & West Point
52. Florida, Atlantic & Gulf Central
53. Florida R. R.
54. Pensacola & Georgia
55. Tallahassee R. R.
56. Alabama & Florida R. R. of Fla.
57. Alabama & Florida R. R. of Ala.
58. Montgomery & Eufaula
59. Montgomery & West Point
60. Tuskegee R. R.
61. Mobile & Girard
62. Mobile & Great Northern
63. Spring Hill R. R.
64. Mobile & Ohio
65. Mississippi, Gainesville & Tuscaloosa
66. Memphis & Charleston
67. Wills Valley
68. Nashville & Chattanooga
69. Winchester & Alabama
70. McMinnville & Manchester
71. Tennessee & Alabama
72. Nashville & Northwestern
73. Louisville & Nashville
74. Memphis, Clarksville & Louisville
75. Edgefield & Kentucky
76. East Tennessee & Georgia
77. East Tennessee & Virginia
78. Knoxville & Kentucky
79. Rogersville & Jefferson
80. Memphis & Ohio
81. Northeast & Southwest
82. Alabama & Mississippi Rivers
83. Cahaba, Marion & Greensboro
84. New Orleans & Ohio
85. Mississippi Central
86. Mississippi & Tennessee
87. Memphis & Little Rock

88. New Orleans, Jackson & Great Northern
89. Southern R. R. of Mississippi
90. Raymond R. R.
91. Jefferson & Lake Pontchartrain
92. Pontchartrain R. R.
93. Mexican Gulf R. R.
94. New Orleans, Opelousas & Great Western
95. West Feliciana R. R.
96. Clinton & Port Hudson
97. Baton Rouge, Grosse Tete & Opelousas
98. Vicksburg, Shreveport & Texas
99. Alexandria & Cheneyville
100. Texas & New Orleans
101. Eastern Texas R. R.
102. Buffalo Bayou, Brazos & Colorado
103. Houston Tap & Brazoria
104. Galveston, Houston & Henderson
105. Houston & Texas Central
106. Washington County R. R.
107. San Antonio & Mexican Gulf
108. Memphis, El Paso & Pacific
109. Southern Pacific
110. Manassas Gap
111. Alabama & Tennessee Rivers
112. Hungary Branch
113. Grand Gulf & Port Gibson

The Railro
The Confedera

AS OF JUNE 1, 18

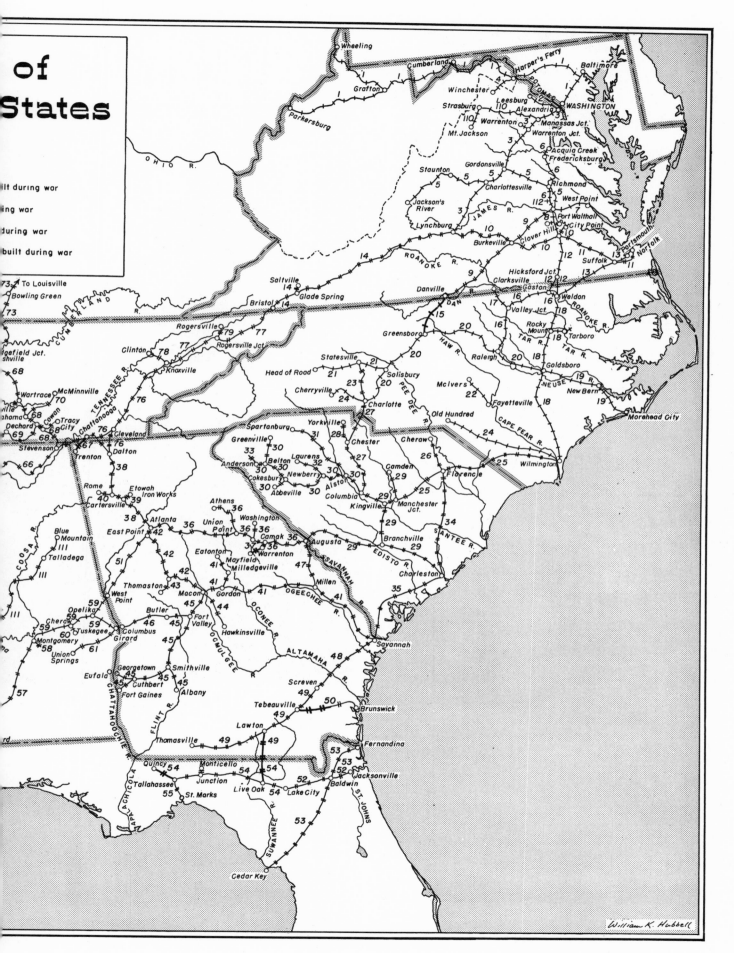

of

States

lt during war

ing war

during war

built during war

War! War!--To Arms!

Fighting has commenced at several points, and Northern troops are moving Southward by the thousand! Let us prepare to meet the enemy at once! We must make sacrifices or be overwhelmed by our enemies! A large number of volunteers are called for from Alabama, and if not raised speedily, a draft may be expected. Let it not be said that men have to be drafted in Clarke County.

At a meeting of the old members of the Grove Hill Guards, on last Saturday, about 50 of them declared themselves ready, and formed a temporary organization. More of them will join the company; but about 30 recruits are needed to complete the ranks of the company. A meeting of the company will be held next Saturday at Grove Hill, at which time it is proposed to organize the company permanently.

Come forward, fellow citizens, and respond to your country's call!

Capt. J. M. Hall will address the citizens of Choctaw Corner on Wednesday, April 24th, and the citizens of Coffeeville on Friday, April 26, where recruits may attach themselves to the Company.

Grove Hill, April 22, '61.

Clarke County Democrat, April 22, 1861

Alabama Department of Archives and His[tory]

A TYPICAL ALABAMA VOLUNTEER OF '61. In the first months of the war men rushed to volunteer, afraid the war would be over before they could serve. Many of the uniforms were homemade, and swords were sometimes fashioned from wagon-wheel rims.

WAR IN ALABAMA

Alabama seceded from the Union January 11, 1861, the fourth state to secede. In a spirit of adventure men rushed to volunteer, afraid that the war would be over before they could serve. Governor A. B. Moore, convinced that the war would last only a few months, prophesied that there would be a grand march to Washington. Secretary of War LeRoy Pope Walker said in a Montgomery speech, "The flag which now flaunts the breeze will float over the dome of the old Capitol at Washington before the first of May." During 1861 twenty-eight regiments of infantry and one regiment of cavalry were organized in Alabama.

As the weeks passed, however, the Federal plan of action became clear, and hopes for a short war faded. Confederate ports, including Mobile, were blockaded to curtail cotton exports. Union battle lines were divided into two sections—the Eastern Army, designed to capture and occupy Richmond, and the Western, to strike against the Mississippi river and the lower Southern states to prevent food and supplies being sent to the Confederate armies. In the heart of the lower South was Alabama, flanked on three sides by Georgia, Tennessee, and Mississippi, which protected her from major battles throughout the war.

From a population of not much more than half a million Alabama sent 125,000 men to fight with the Confederate States of America, which meant that about one of every four Alabamians fought with the Confederacy. Of these 125,000 Alabama soldiers, approximately 30,000 died in the war.

In addition to supplying soldiers, Alabama furnished raw materials and manufactured goods for the Confederate States. When the war started, ninety-five percent of the people in Alabama lived on farms. They were too busy as cotton planters, large and small, to be concerned with industry. They bought plows made in Pennsylvania, clothes from New York, salt from the West Indies. Now all that was changed. There would be no more trade with the North or any other part of the world except by the blockade runners, as the Federals had sealed off the Southern ports. The South must produce or die.

Long buried in Alabama's hill country lay an inexhaustible supply of coal and iron ore, but not until the Civil War was iron made in Alabama in any quantity. As furnace after furnace was fired in, Alabama became the largest producer of iron for the Confederacy. Sixteen blast furnaces turned out an average of 219 tons per day. The largest producers were at Oxmoor, Irondale, Tannehill, and Brierfield. Six rolling mills took the iron and shaped it for production. The largest rolling mill was located at Selma, the manufacturing center of the state. Scattered throughout Alabama, however, were tanneries, hat factories, harness shops, cotton mills, and many machine and work shops. At Montgomery the Alabama Arms Manufacturing Company produced Enfield rifles.

After the Ordinance of Secession, Governor A. B. Moore assumed control of the Federal arsenal at Mount Vernon, near Mobile. With the fall of New Orleans in 1862, General Josiah Gorgas, chief of the Confederate Ordnance Department, ordered the arsenal moved to a less vulnerable inland location at Selma. The Confederate States of America employed about ten thousand skilled workers at the Selma arsenal munitions works. These ten thousand laborers manufactured cannons, small arms, and munitions. Selma built the ships that met Farragut

(Continued)

This old lathe on the campus at Auburn University was used in the manufacture of ammunition in Selma during the Civil War. A secondhand machinery dealer bought it after the war and sold it to the Linn Iron works in Birmingham. Just as it was about to be shipped to Japan as scrap iron, its history came to light.

Decatur was captured and recaptured by both Union and Confederate troops. Only three buildings survived the war intact. This sketch was made by a Federal soldier with the Third Ohio Volunteers.

REMAINS OF OLD TANNEHILL
FURNACE SOUTH OF BESSEMER.
*This furnace supplied the Confederacy
not only with the munitions of war such
as cannon balls and gun barrels, but
also with pots, pans, and skillets. It was
destroyed by Wilson's raiders in 1865.*

at Mobile Bay—the ironclad *Tennessee,* and the gunboats *Selma, Morgan,* and *Gaines.* All the ships were mounted with guns made at the Selma foundry, charged with powder and ball from the arsenal. Commander Roger ap C. Jones, C. S. N., chief of ordnance works at Selma, supervised construction of these Confederate ships.

Another vital product found in Alabama was salt. After the Port of Mobile was closed, the Confederacy sought a source of supply within its own borders. Soon saltworks appeared in Clarke, Baldwin, Mobile, and Washington counties. Entire families, many with slaves, came to the saltworks and pitched camp so that they could make enough salt for their winter's use. The army, as well as civilians, needed salt for the curing of meats.

Not only did the Confederacy in its eleven states have to meet all the necessities of a civilian and military population, it had to carry commodities from state to state and to the battle lines. At the outbreak of the war Alabama had only 643 miles of railroad track, built at a cost of $26,845. She depended largely upon her natural waterways for transportation. Cotton was floated down the rivers to the markets, and steamboats carried passengers. In war, however, men and supplies must be moved, and as

quickly as possible. Typical of the transportation problem in Alabama was that of the 28th Alabama Regiment. It was raised in Jefferson county in March of 1862 in response to General Albert Sidney Johnston's plea for reinforcements to hold back the Federals pushing toward Corinth. Since there was no railroad through the central part of the state to carry the troops directly to Corinth, the 28th Alabama had to travel in wagons and by boats south to Mobile, instead of west to Corinth. In Mobile they boarded the northbound cars of the Mobile and Ohio Railroad and arrived in Corinth the day after the Confederate defeat, too late to stop the Federal troops from invading north Alabama.

As the Confederates retreated after Shiloh and Corinth, north Alabama opened to Federal troops. In April of 1862 General O. M. Mitchell occupied Huntsville, and General I. V. Turchinov captured Athens. From that time on the Federal army marched back and forth across northern Alabama—raiding, burning, and capturing Confederate supplies. The Federal army was also successful in recruiting Union sympathizers. By the fall of 1864 there were many of these sympathizers, some of them deserters from the Confederate army hiding in the mountains of north Alabama. They raided the sur-

(Continued)

TRAIN WITH REINFORCEMENTS FOR GENERAL JOHNSTON RUNS OFF THE TRACK. *On railroad cars such as these the 28th Alabama Regiment arrived too late for the Battle of Corinth. Frank Vizetelly, a strongly pro-Southern artist-correspondent for the ILLUSTRATED LONDON NEWS, made this sketch while traveling with the troop train on the Charleston and Memphis Railroad. During the Civil War newspapers and magazines found that sketches by combat artists were easier and less expensive to use than photography, still a new art. Such drawings, frequently made on the field of battle, were sometimes highly romanticized; nevertheless they furnish an invaluable record.*

General Joseph Wheeler

Mississippi, Gainesville & Tuskaloosa Railroad. -

OFFICE IN GAINESVILLE,
27th May, 1862.

ON and after Monday next, the second day of June, Daily Freight and Passenger Trains will run on this road as follows :

Leave Gainesville at 4 P. M., arrive at Gainesville Junction at 6 P. M. Leave the Junction at 7 A. M., and arrive at Gainesville at 9 A. M. Connections made with the Mobile & Ohio Road, and Stages running East.

A. K. RAMSEY.

General John Tyler Morgan

Mobile belle Kate Cumming became a Confederate nurse and hospital matron. Her book A JOURNAL OF HOSPITAL LIFE IN THE CONFEDERATE ARMY OF TENNESSEE, published in 1866, was among the first of the printed records of women's roles in the war. This journal recounts her life behind the lines where her duties ranged from writing letters for the disabled and preparing diets for the sick, to closing the eyes of the dead.

rounding countryside, seizing food and supplies.

Alabama defended its soil with raids and counter raids into surrounding enemy-occupied territory. This called for fast-moving cavalrymen and skilled cavalry leaders. General Joseph Wheeler of Lawrence county was one of the most daring and successful cavalry officers of the Confederacy. A West Point graduate, Wheeler resigned from the United States army to become a lieutenant of artillery in the Confederate States army. As a result of his command of the 19th Alabama Infantry at Shiloh, he was promoted to brigadier general, and in June, 1862, he organized the cavalry of the Army of the Mississippi.

In 1863-64 General Wheeler struck successfully against the Army of the Cumberland at Mumford, Murphreesboro, and Chickamauga. One of the most daring cavalry raids was against the Federal supply depot at Bridgeport, Alabama. Because of the loss of ammunition and provisions as a result of General Wheeler's raid, General Rosecrans was forced to place his army on starvation rations and was not able to move out of Chattanooga toward Georgia as planned.

It is estimated that General Wheeler during the Civil War had eighteen horses shot from under him, that he fought in one hundred twenty-seven battles, and that he engaged in five hundred additional skirmishes.

Another important cavalryman from Alabama was General John Tyler Morgan of Selma. In 1862 Morgan recruited and organized the 51st Alabama Cavalry. Under Morgan's command this regiment was active in northern Alabama protecting the railroads and the people. General Morgan served with both Wheeler and Forrest.

The cavalryman that gave the Federals the most trouble in Alabama, as well as in Mississippi, Tennessee, and Georgia, was "that devil" Nathan Bedford Forrest. When the Civil War started, Forrest enlisted as a private in June, 1861. He had been a successful cotton planter in Memphis, Tennessee. Forrest had a natural genius for military tactics. He quickly rose from a rank of private. After the Battle of Chickamauga he made major general, and later lieutenant general. Forrest, discarding many of the conventional cavalry tactics, brought his men into battle as mounted infantry. Wounded many times, Forrest liked to be in the thick of the fighting and is said to have killed more of the enemy in hand-to-hand combat than any other general. He was reported to have had twenty-nine horses shot from under him.

(Continued)

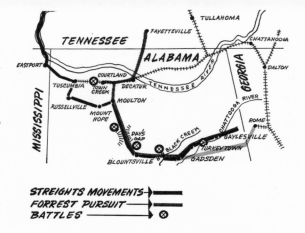

Owsley, Know Alabama, Colonial Press

STREIGHTS MOVEMENTS ⟶
FORREST PURSUIT ⟶
BATTLES ⟶ ⊗

Streight's Route Across Alabama

Major General Nathan Bedford Forrest

One of the boldest and most significant raids into Alabama was that of Colonel A. D. Streight in 1863. Streight's aim was to cut the railroads leading out of Chattanooga in one direction to Knoxville and in the other to Atlanta. With two thousand picked men Colonel Streight filed out of Eastport, Mississippi, just over the Alabama border, on April 23, 1863. He had mounted most of his men on mules, for mules could best cross the rocky mountains over which the troops would travel. His route lay almost due east across a sparsely populated region of northern Alabama. There were many Union sympathizers in this area, and Streight did not expect opposition from the local citizenry.

Opposing Streight was General Nathan Bedford Forrest, who set out from Fayetteville, Tennessee, with one thousand men to catch Streight and protect the railroads. At Courtland, Alabama, Forrest began a ride that is remarkable in military history. From April 29 to May 1 the Confederate troops pursued Streight's raiders. When the Confederates reached Blountsville, they had ridden fifty-seven hours and fought two major engagements, one on Sand Mountain and one at Gay's Gap. After a brief rest in Blountsville, Forrest continued the pursuit to Gadsden and on to Lawrence, where Streight at last surrendered. Forrest's troops had dwindled to about six hundred, and to this small force Colonel Streight surrendered what was left of the two thousand picked troops that had started from Nashville on April 10.

Forrest had ridden so close on the heels of Streight that Streight believed himself pursued by overwhelming numbers. Forrest shipped his Union prisoners to Richmond via the railroad they had come to destroy.

A well-known story in Alabama is that of Emma Sansom and General Nathan Bedford Forrest. As General Streight moved across Alabama, he burned the bridge at Gadsden over Black creek to delay Forrest, close on his heels. When Forrest saw the bridge in flames, he sought a guide to show him where the creek could be forded. Fifteen-year-old Emma Sansom volunteered, and she safely led Forrest and his men and horses across the creek. When a bullet pierced her dress, she defiantly waved her bonnet at the enemy. The Federals were so impressed with her bravery they ceased firing.

Major John Pelham

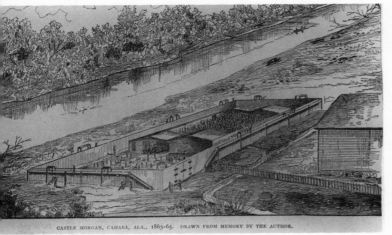

CASTLE MORGAN, CAHABA, ALA., 1863-65. DRAWN FROM MEMORY BY THE AUTHOR.

The number of prisoners through the winter of 1864-1865 was three thousand—five times more crowded than Andersonville.

SOBER REFLECTIONS IN '63

In 1863, the war's middle year, Alabamians were having sober reflections. Forgotten were those early days of optimism concerning Northern unwillingness to fight. Union forces were capturing and occupying north Alabama, including Huntsville, Decatur, and Florence. The North could no longer allow Alabama to be the Confederacy's "heart." Targets must include furnaces and factories at Huntsville, Decatur, and Florence. In due time the more Southern cities of Montgomery, Selma, and Mobile must fall. In addition, the Confederacy's prison camp at Cahaba must be taken.

Amid these troubles Alabama needed a young war hero and found him in the "Gallant Pelham." Born near Alexandria, Alabama, John Pelham, just graduating from West Point at the time of Alabama's secession, slipped through the Federal lines in Kentucky, passing as a secret agent of General Winfield Scott. He hurried to Montgomery, where the new Confederate government was being organized, and he immediately received a commission as lieutenant from the Confederate Secretary of War, Leroy Pope Walker. Pelham's fearless fighting with one cannon in the Battle of Fredericksburg impressed Lee so much that he addressed the youth as the "gallant Pelham," and the nickname stuck. Pelham was killed in action March 17, 1863, at the age of twenty-four.

223

Federal Forces Occupy North Alabama

General John A. Logan, commander of Federal forces in north Alabama, poses in Napoleonic manner with his commander in chief, General William T. Sherman.

Many Confederate shoulders were sagging by 1864. In such Alabama areas as Stevenson, Union troops by this year were moving about freely. The dividing line was the Tennessee river, with Federals in control north of that line. Early in 1864 Union General John A. Logan established a major headquarters in Huntsville.

At Stevenson, Alabama, in Jackson county, the Nashville, Chattanooga, and St. Louis Railway connected with the Memphis and Charleston. Stevenson was headquarters for the Union Army Command from the time of the battle at Chickamauga in 1862 through the battles of Atlanta and of Nashville in 1864. The Alabama House, a three-story frame building with fifty rooms, housed the Union forces.

Stevenson, Alabama, occupied by Federal troops

THE ARMY OF THE CUMBERLAND—STEVENSON

This woodcut depicting Huntsville in 1864 shows in lower foreground the McDowell-LaVert-Chase home that was headquarters in 1862 for Union General O. M. Mitchell and in 1864 for Union General John A. Logan.

By April in Huntsville Southern belles were dancing the "Virginia Reel" with Federal soldiers and otherwise hobnobbing with the enemy.

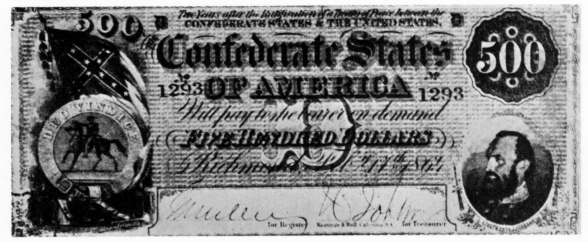

The Confederate states issued their own money, and thousands of people lost everything when the money system collapsed with the Confederacy.

FADING HOPES

As 1864 advanced, so did Union forces, and with them fading Confederate hopes. Typical of such misfortune was the fate of a once-dashing Raphael Semmes. Admiral Semmes, who resigned as an admiral in the United States Navy to protect the South, rode his commerce raider, the *Alabama,* until Union forces sank it off Cherbourg, France, in June, 1864.

Confederate money, so popular at the start, was less valuable now. Some Alabamians were beginning to realize that they soon would lose everything if the money system collapsed with the Confederacy. Their possessions and their government depended upon each other.

A needed ray of hope was Confederate Colonel James Jackson's raid north across the Tennessee river on April 11, 1864. Jackson and members of his regiment could look from their encampment north across the Tennessee river toward their captured homes. Jackson's father

had built the Forks of Cypress near Florence, and his widowed mother still lived there. A sensitive, complex officer, Jackson once angrily ordered his command to "fix bayonets and charge," to frighten a Confederate Georgia regiment from destroying flowers and shrubbery at a Mississippi plantation home. Now, alarmed by Federals near the Forks of Cypress, Jackson selected 150 men and one night rowed across the Tennessee river at Tuscumbia, landing near Florence. A captured Negro slave reluctantly guided Jackson to a Federal "White Horse Company" near the Forks. Attacking this same night, with his men shouting "Forrest! Forrest!" to scare the Yankees, Jackson captured forty-two prisoners, forty-four large white horses, and turned loose many steers claimed by the Federals. Hearing of "devil Forrest" nearby, some Federal troops fled into Tennessee. Around the campfires in the lean months ahead Confederates recounted the daring raid.

226

Admiral Raphael Semmes was described by those who knew him as a stiffly erect handsome man with piercing black eyes and a pointed waxed mustache. This painting by Maltby Sykes hangs in the Alabama Department of Archives and History.

A rare photograph of Admiral Semmes, seated, and Commander Kell taken in England after the sinking of the ALABAMA. They are shown here with their hostesses, who helped to rescue them from the English Channel.

As the ALABAMA sinks in the English Channel, the lifeboat hurries to the rescue of the crew. From a drawing in BLUEJACKETS OF '61 published in 1884.

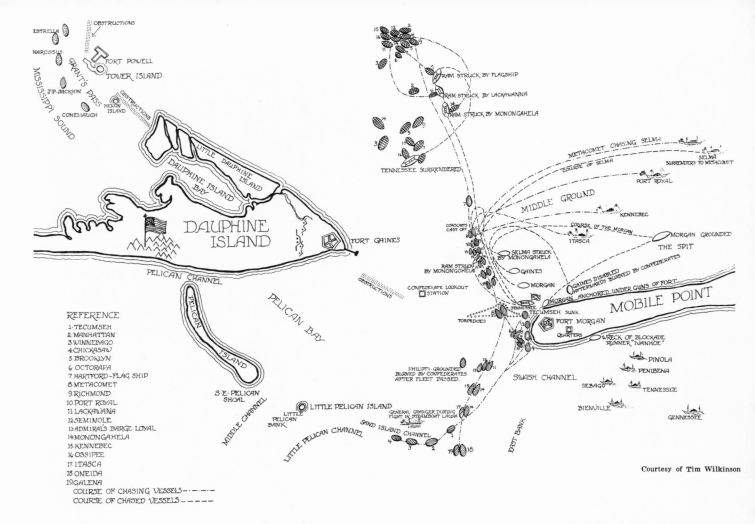

Courtesy of Tim Wilkinson

This photograph made immediately after the capture of Fort Gaines shows Admiral Farragut in the fort discussing with General Gordon Granger plans for the attack by which Fort Morgan was taken August 22, 1864.

Admiral Franklin Buchanan conferring with Captain Tattnall, commander of the MERRIMAC. Admiral Buchanan was the highest ranking officer in the Confederate navy and had been the first commander of the United States Naval Academy.

Battle of Mobile Bay

After the capture of New Orleans in 1862, Mobile became the only seaport on the Gulf of Mexico into which the Confederacy could ship arms, medicines, and other supplies, and out of which it could ship cotton. Union forces attempted to blockade the port, but until the Battle of Mobile Bay many Confederate ships sailed through. Historians and military strategists consider the Battle of Mobile Bay the most important military action in Alabama during the Civil War.

The defeat of the small Confederate flotilla which controlled Mobile Bay was essential. Because of Confederate successes, the Union badly needed a victory, and Admiral Farragut was ordered to take Mobile Bay at all costs.

On each side of the opening between Mobile Bay and the Gulf of Mexico was a Confederate fort, Fort Morgan, on the east, and Fort Gaines, on the west. In addition to their small fleet and the two forts, the Confederates were protecting the opening with 150 mines, or torpedoes. Waiting outside in the Gulf to fight its way in between the two forts and past the torpedoes,

and then to meet the waiting Confederate ships, was a large Union fleet.

Shortly after seven o'clock on the morning of August 5, 1864, Union Admiral David Farragut spoke his famous words, "Damn the torpedoes —full speed ahead," and ordered his fleet to continue north from the Gulf into Mobile Bay. Farragut, with seventeen ships under his command, hoped to make short work of the Confederate fleet, consisting of the C.S.S. *Tennessee* (sister ship to the ironclad *Merrimac)* and three wooden gunboats. The initial threat to Farragut's fleet was Fort Morgan, which was much nearer the channel than Fort Gaines, on Dauphin Island, to the west.

In order to pass the guns of Fort Morgan guarding the entrance to the bay, Farragut threw a screen between his ship and the gunners at the fort by igniting gunpowder on the ship's deck. The smoke was carried to the fort by the prevailing wind. No sooner had Farragut passed the fort, however, than his lead ship, the *Tecumseh*, struck a torpedo and immediately sank. The rest of the fleet passed safely through.

229

"LACKAWANNA."   "OSSIPEE."   "BROOKLYN."   "ITASCA."   "RICHMOND."
"WINNEBAGO."   "TENNESSEE."

Farragut Versus Buchanan

The guns of Fort Morgan had failed to turn back the enemy. The C.S.S. *Tennessee* had already earned itself a nickname of "monster" because it was protected by six inches of iron armor around its most vulnerable part and because it floated in reptilian manner low on the water. Its overworked builders in Selma, however, had been forced to improvise in building the ship and had left it with several fatal faults, including an exposed rudder control and engines too small for the ship's tremendous weight. Undismayed by these faults, Confederate Admiral Franklin Buchanan guided the *Tennessee* forward to lead the Confederate fleet to meet the foe, commanded by an old acquaintance, Union Admiral David G. Farragut. Before war had made them enemies, Farragut had been on familiar terms with Buchanan and called him "old Buck." Within a short time the Union fleet had knocked all three gunboats out of battle, but "old Buck's" lone *Tennessee* fought on.

For four hours the *Tennessee* matched her six guns and two hundred men against seventeen ships, one hundred ninety-nine guns, seven hundred men, and one of the greatest United States admirals of all times. Confederate Admiral Buchanan, who had sworn never to surrender the *Tennessee*, rammed ship after ship. Finally, however, the unequal conflict proved too much for even a man of Buchanan's courage. The armor of the *Tennessee* was penetrated in several places, and at last came the shot that almost fatally wounded Buchanan. With her steering gear shot away, the *Tennessee* surrendered while Buchanan was being treated below deck for a leg injury that luckily did not prove fatal. Thus closed the naval battle that ended Confederate rule on the Gulf Coast and earned for Farragut his proudest laurels.

'ORD." "CHICKASAW."
FORT MORGAN.

231

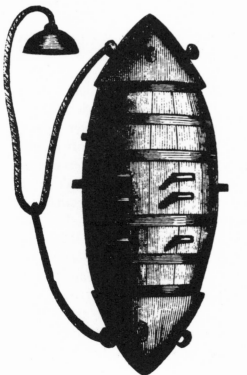

THE COLLISION OF THE HARTFORD AND THE TEN-
NESSEE WITH ADMIRAL FARRAGUT STANDING ON THE
BRIDGE. *A Union officer aboard the* HARTFORD *described the
encounter in this way: "The two flagships approached each other
bow to bow. The two admirals, Farragut and Buchanan, had
entered the Navy together as boys and up to the outbreak of the
war had been warm friends. But now each was hoping for the
overthrow of the other . . . Just as the two vessels were meeting,
the course of the* TENNESSEE *was slightly changed, enough to
strike us only a glancing blow on the port bow, which left us
uninjured, while the two vessels grated past each other. Buchanan
tried to sink us with a broadside as he went by; but only one
of his guns went off, the primers and all the others failing. That
gun sent a shell that entered the berthdeck of the* HARTFORD
and killed five men."

*Torpedoes such as this were laid in the pass of
Mobile Bay to stop Farragut's fleet. Because of
them Farragut ordered, "Damn the torpedoes—full
speed ahead!"*

These magnificent arches are part of Fort Morgan near Gulf Shores, Alabama. The fort is a copy of one designed by Michelangelo and built near Florence, Italy.

This photo shows the five-pointed star design of Fort Morgan, one of the richest historical sites in America.

The Capture of Fort Morgan

With the end of the Battle of Mobile Bay, Union forces were able to capture Fort Gaines and Fort Powell, but Fort Morgan refused to surrender. Farragut landed forty cannon and twelve thousand soldiers to attack Fort Morgan from land while the fleet shelled it from the sea. From August 5 to August 23 Fort Morgan was under constant bombardment, and finally it began to burn. On the morning of August 23 Brigadier General R. L. Page raised the white flag of surrender. Admiral Farragut had successfully sealed off Mobile Bay to blockade runners, although it would be eight months before the capture of the city of Mobile by Union troops.

233

A Union guard stands on duty in front of the main barracks. The disastrous effects of the shells exploding inside the fort can be seen.

Photographs on these two pages were made by a photographer from Admiral Farragut's fleet. They show the destruction at Fort Morgan after a nineteen-day siege.

The Battle of Fort Morgan, which lasted nineteen days, took its toll of the old Mobile Point Lighthouse. The little tower in the distance is a temporary lighthouse erected by Admiral Farragut for his own quick use.

234

This view depicts Union soldiers in the arena with the "Stars and Stripes" flying over the captured fort.

...ast of Fort Morgan can be seen the little Confederate village, ...here the officers, wives, and children of the garrison lived. The ...ndbags and cannon are on the northeast part of the fort.

Union soldiers rest on a gun emplacement inside Fort Morgan. A shell has partly destroyed the sandbag wall to the left. A civilian leaning on the gun at right views the aftermath.

Wilson's raiders are shown here putting Jefferson Davis in an ambulance after capturing him near Irwinville, Georgia, on May 10, 1865. Davis was making his way to Alabama to join the last remnants of the Confederate forces.

THE FATAL YEAR OF '65

By January 1865, Confederate resistance on all fronts was collapsing before the driving Federal armies. Sherman had taken Atlanta; Federals were attacking Petersburg and Richmond; and Thomas in the West had annihilated Hood's army in Tennessee with devastating victories at Franklin and Nashville.

Grant now eyed the remainder of the wounded Confederacy. To twenty-eight-year-old Brevet Major General James H. Wilson, one of the Federal army's bright new stars, went the task of capturing the Confederacy's heart. Wilson had already proved himself as commander of Sherman's cavalry; now, for his invasion of Alabama and Georgia he assembled the most formidable mounted force in the Federal army. Grant suggested taking only 5,000 men into "Forrest's back yard," but Wilson persuaded him to authorize 13,500 officers and men for the invasion. Not until mid-March was Wilson able to ford the flood-swollen Tennessee to begin his advance. Hoping to deceive his opponents concerning his intentions, he marched in three separate columns until he was out of the mountainous country of north Alabama.

Meanwhile, from his headquarters at West Point, Mississippi, Forrest learned of the invasion and directed Jackson to try to delay Wilson at Tuscaloosa. Forrest himself would move to a stronger defensive position at Plantersville, fifteen miles north of Selma. Forrest had less than 10,000 men scattered over a wide area for the protection of Alabama. Vulnerable points along Wilson's path, such as Tuscaloosa and the University of Alabama, must rely for protection on elderly men and children plus a few young cadets at the university. Part of Wilson's invading force under Brigadier General Croxton destroyed Tuscaloosa and most of the university, before Jackson's force could arrive to aid them.

Simultaneously Wilson sent another advance force, Upton's 4th Division, to repulse Forrest and twice defeat a small unit at Montevallo, forty miles north of Selma. Upton's men were jubilant that a Federal general at last had been able to "get the bulge" on Forrest.

WILSON'S RAIDERS ON THE MOVE

On April 4, 1865, while Federal troops were burning most of the University of Alabama, faculty wives formed a bucket brigade and put out the fire to save from destruction the Little Round House, shown here. When the university adopted military discipline in 1860, it erected for the officer on duty this small Norman tower at the corner of the original university quadrangle.

Here is Major General Harrison Wilson, seated in chair at left, with his staff. His cavalry, known as Wilson's raiders, swept over many Alabama counties raiding smokehouses, chicken yards, and hog pens, and destroying all forges, furnaces, mills, and industrial establishments. In twenty-eight days near the end of the war Wilson's raiders captured 288 guns and 6,280 prisoners including Jefferson Davis. They destroyed five large iron works, three factories, numerous mills and large quantities of supplies.

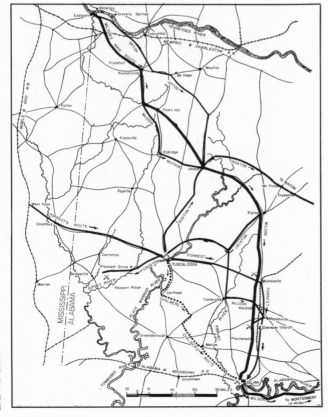

Route of Wilson's Raid Through Alabama

A VIEW OF SELMA, DRAWN MAY 24, 1865. Following Selma's destruction, artists, photographers, and reporters described its aftermath.

THE SACK OF SELMA

By late afternoon on April 2, 1865, the same day Richmond was surrendering to Grant, Union General Wilson was observing Selma, having come three hundred miles in twelve days. Forrest, Armstrong, Abraham Buford, and the rest fought frantically, but as at Montevallo and Ebenezer Church the Federals moved forward. Selma that night saw Confederates in full retreat, and a victorious Federal soldier saw Selma as one of the worst horrors of war, "with a captured city burning at night, a victorious army advancing, and a demoralized one retreating."

The loss of Selma staggered an already crumbling Confederacy and was good reason for Federal rejoicing. There were 2,700 Confederate prisoners, 102 pieces of artillery, and hundreds of horses plus stockpiles of war supplies.

Wilson proceeded promptly to Montgomery, and without a shot occupied the city on April 12th. Appomattox was now three days old, but Wilson lacked official word. After Selma fell, Columbus, Georgia, was the Confederacy's last major manufacturing center and storehouse. As at Selma and Montgomery, Wilson destroyed everything of military value, stopping only at official word of Lee's surrender.

According to present-day Selma residents, these are "Yankee ale bottles" retrieved from Beech creek, Selma. Local historians agree that Yankee invaders drank ale from these bottles and threw them into the creek on their way to fight the Battle of Selma.

RUINS OF CONFEDERATE NAVAL FOUNDRY, SELMA, BURNED APRIL 5, 1865. Because Selma was the site of the great arsenal and naval foundry and the converging point for war supplies for a vast portion of the South, it was considered by the Confederate war department the most important point in Alabama to defend. A desperate effort was made to fortify and defend it, but heavy rains made it impossible to finish the fortifications and to move troops, wagons, and artillery with safety. Thus, all the early plans for the defense of Selma miscarried, and the city, overcome by a more powerful adversary, fell prey to the torch of the Federal troops.

Arsenal Place, at the intersection of Water avenue and Church street in Selma, commemorates the site of the Confederate army's three-square-block Selma Arsenal. The marker states: "These ordnance works stood second only to those of Richmond in the manufacture of the war materials for the Confederate States of America. The work of the several thousand men, women, and children who served at the arsenal has passed into history." On April 6, 1865, the Union army destroyed this Selma Arsenal, terminating the efforts of the "several thousand men, women and children."

THE LAST BATTLE

While General Wilson raided central Alabama, the last sizable campaign of the Civil War was taking place around Mobile. Federal General E. R. S. Canby had been ordered to take Mobile at all costs and had been supplied with about forty-seven thousand men for the campaign. After the successful capture of Fort Gaines and Fort Morgan in the Battle of Mobile Bay some nine months previously, only two Confederate strongholds stood in General Canby's way. They were Spanish Fort, directly across the bay from Mobile, and Fort Blakely, ten miles northeast of Mobile at the junction of the Appalachee and Tensaw rivers. Canby organized his men into two columns. He moved thirty-two thousand men from Fort Gaines and Fort Morgan to the mouth of the Fish river and from there along the edge of the river to Spanish Fort and Fort Blakely. The other column of thirteen thousand men, commanded by General Frederick Steel, marched from Pensacola to cut the Mobile and Montgomery Railroad and stop any Confederate troops from attempting to aid Mobile.

Fort Blakely was important to the defense of Mobile. On April 9, the day that Lee surrendered, the costly siege of Fort Blakely took place. At the fort were twenty-seven thousand men, all seasoned veterans, commanded by General St. John Liddell. Fort Blakely was well fortified, its flanks resting in the marshes of the Appalachee river. The approach to the fort was guarded by trenches, advanced rifle pits, and many pieces of artillery. These withheld the enemy for several hours as enemy forces slowly fought their way to the fort. However, by nightfall, after a day of fierce fighting, Fort Blakely was overrun. About two thousand Federal troops were killed or wounded. Twenty-four hundred Confederates were taken prisoners, and three hundred were killed.

Commanding the Confederate defense of Mobile was Confederate General D. H. Maury with only about nine thousand men under his command, many of them young boys and old men. Although the city was strongly fortified with earthworks, forts, and cannon, the Confederates were outnumbered eight to one. With the fall of Fort Blakely it was no longer possible to defend Mobile, and three days after that important battle General Maury with about forty-five hundred soldiers withdrew to Meridian, and Federal forces at last occupied Mobile.

Finally on May 6 Forrest surrendered at Gainesville, Alabama, and on May 9 he made his farewell speech to his men. Speaking with homely eloquence, he said: "That we are beaten is a self-evident fact . . . the armies of Lee and

THE LANDING OF FEDERAL FORCES FROM FORT MORGAN AT FISH RIVER BELOW MOBILE ON MARCH 23, 24 and 28, 1865. They were part of the attack on the city of Mobile.

Johnston having surrendered, you are the last of all the troops of the C. S. A. east of the Mississippi to lay down your arms . . . I have never on a field of battle sent you where I was unwilling to go myself, nor would I now advise you to a course which I felt myself unwilling to pursue. You have been good soldiers, you can now be good citizens . . . Obey the laws, preserve your honour."

Alabamians would long remember the dead and wounded, smoke from burning houses, rubble heaps of destroyed furnaces, and stench of rotting animal carcasses as Federal forces swept the state. But most Alabamians lowered the Confederate flag willingly and accepted the example of leaders such as Lee and Forrest as they set about rebuilding a wrecked homeland.

On April 19, 1865, with the capture of the town of Blakely by Federal troops, the last defense of Mobile disappeared. Federal troops occupied Mobile April 12, 1865, in the last days of the Confederacy; General Robert E. Lee had already surrendered.

241

IN MEMORY OF A LOST CAUSE

In half a decade Alabama fell from a proud Southern state to defeat. Union soldiers had invaded the homeland, had burned private homes as well as public buildings, and had killed many men and boys. Only Grant's generous terms to Lee at Appomattox, and Lee's far-sighted refusal to turn his army into guerilla warriors, had brought a small measure of hope. As it was, Alabama and other Southern states had bitter memories that lingered long.

The hardships Jefferson Davis endured in Northern prisons for two years after the war helped place him at the pinnacle of a Confederate "Hall of Fame." When Davis died, on December 6, 1889, Southern compatriots buried him in beautiful Metairie Cemetery outside New Orleans. During the next four years, however, popular opinion in the South was demanding that Davis have a permanent resting place at Richmond, Virginia, the last capital of the Confederacy. This feeling resulted in the removal of his remains from Metairie in 1893.

The Confederate monuments found in most Alabama towns a[r]e popular gathering places for observance of Confederate Memoria[l] Day. Here in Livingston, near the turn of the century, t[he] group of children dressed in their "Sunday best" pose for th[e] picture while Confederate flags fly at the base of the monumen[t]

Huntsville Times

In Huntsville twenty-five years after the war these Confederate veterans met to remember. The war brought tragedy to almost as many homes of Alabama citizens as it missed. Those remaining did not forget.

242

Confederate monument in Live Oak Cemetery at Selma. At the base of the monument are the names of Selma's dead in the war. Many Confederate memorial ceremonies have been held at this site. Nearby is a stone chair that the "Ladies of Selma" have dedicated to the memory of Confederate President Jefferson Davis.

This monument to Jefferson Davis erected by the United Daughters of the Confederacy stands on the capitol grounds in Montgomery. Names of the seceding states are carved around the base.

In Montgomery on May 21, 1893, the bier with the remains of Davis passes through the Alabama capital enroute to Richmond for final interment in Richmond's Hollywood Cemetery beside the James river. In Montgomery Davis's remains lay in state overnight at the capitol, and thousands of Alabamians filed past to pay final respect.

243

Index

Boldface numbers refer to captions or pictures.

244

DATE DUE

PRINTED IN U.S.A.